Benjamin

**ANNALISA MENIN**
**SUSANNA DE CIECHI**

# MY LAST YEAR IN NEW YORK

Original title: Il mio ultimo anno a New York
© 2017 – Annalisa Menin and Susanna De Ciechi
e-mail: menin.deciechi@gmail.com

Translation from the Italian: Alastair McEwen

ISBN: 978-0692974162

Editing: Amanda West
Layout: Serena Zonca www.autopubblicarsi.it
Cover artwork: Virginia Cedrini

Note

This is a novel and, as such, the idea around which it revolves springs from some events that really occurred, but which have been transfigured and fictionalized. Consequently, the characters, their personalities and the events that involve them are solely the fruit of the authors' creativity and all references to actual names, persons, places, and situations are purely coincidental.

*To Marco*
– Your princess

*My life is in the narration of it
and my memory is fixed with writing;
what I do not put into words on paper
is erased by time.*
– Isabelle Allende


*Who knows if one day, on looking into the eyes
of the one who will have you after me,
you will find something that belongs to me.*
– Pablo Neruda

# CONTENTS

# 1
## SOLSTICE IN MANHATTAN

*New York, May 29, 2016*

"Come on, come on, come on!" I hiss between clenched teeth as I zigzag through the crowd, skirting Bryant Park on Sixth Avenue, heading uptown. I'm hurrying to get to the corner of 42nd street and I stop in front of Starbucks. The road is packed with all kinds of vehicles, on two, four and even six wheels. It is a disorderly torrent rolling north. Horns and yells rise above the background noise, a mix of roaring engines and squealing brakes, music, slammed doors, and footsteps of varying loudness and tone. The first day of summer is heading toward dusk wrapped in a pall of smog. Everyone, apart from the oblivious tourists, is waiting for the marvel for which they have rushed into the streets.

"We could use a little wind," says a young blonde woman in jeans and a T-shirt, who has stopped beside me. A small boy standing in front of her leans his back against her and she wraps her arms around him. He is seven, maybe eight years old. As if she had summoned it, a hot breeze comes up and moves the layer of compact dust suspended in the air.

"Mom, the wind!" The boy throws his head back and his eyes meet his mother's. Their smiles are identical: the shape of their mouths, the gap between their teeth, even the way they crinkle their noses. As he laughs and turns to look toward the far end of the avenue, she hugs him even closer and sways from side to side, taking her son with her in her dance.

The gusts are strong and steady, the traffic is less heavy, the people on the street slow down, and many stop: New York is about to raise the curtain on Manhattanhenge, the moment when the sunset is parallel with 42nd Street and the light fans out over much of Manhattan. Thousands of people are hypnotized by the sight of the orb going down on the horizon. A blaze of light, a summer spectacle that New York grants only twice a year.

The blonde woman bends over to kiss her child's hair. I can't resist watching them as I run my hand over my flat belly. I caress myself to confirm the absence of any promise. "There's nothing in there," I think. "It's all dark, a child would be afraid." All around, people are admiring the glimmering play of light. The mother beside me holds out her arm and points toward the light and her son's gaze darts out, following her finger. It seems to me that everyone is in the company of someone, especially mothers with their children.

I, too, want a child—with Marco. I want it for me, even though I know he doesn't agree. We've been talking about it for years. In that time, the scales of the pros and cons have tilted this way and that, without ever reaching equilibrium. The child, our child, could have come along by chance, but decided to give us time.

But time is not infinite, as light is.

Dusk falls over Manhattan in a heartbeat, the way it does in the tropics.

"Let's go, honey." The blonde woman laces her fingers into her son's, gives me a nod and disappears into the crowd that has started to flow again.

It is the end of a gigantic flash mob; now everything is in motion once more. Only I remain frozen on this street corner, lost in a desperate desire to go back to when Marco saw me as a *mom*. I walk along the edge of the sidewalk, one foot in front of the other without leaving the curb. A game, a wish. There was a time when, if I managed to keep my balance on this imaginary beam, I would have rewarded myself with something sweet, like an ice cream.

What do I want to reward myself with today?

Perhaps I might even make that baby now.

Now that Marco doesn't want one anymore.

He had been the first to come up with the idea. It was a few months after we got married, at the end of 2010.

"Listen, Annina, how about trying for a baby?" He came out with it just like that, on an ordinary morning as we were having breakfast. Marco was sitting sideways on the red kitchen stool as he scooped out the last of the Nutella from the jar with his finger. I carried on sipping my tea.

"So, how do you feel about becoming a mom?" I saw from his narrowed eyes, bordered by the little lines that defined his *responsible* look, that he wasn't about to let it go.

"Yes. We can think about it." I was on the defensive—I was only twenty-seven at that time, but I gave a complaisant smile. I let the minutes go by amid his words, my thoughts and my replies: what I would have liked to say and what I actually would say.

"I can already imagine the three of us, having breakfast around this bar. But not like those schmaltzy ads with happy families! Our baby would be in his high chair spitting all over his bib..."

"Oh, nice! So, that's how you plan to raise your son?"

"Then we're agreed: we'll have a boy. The first will be a boy. Good girl, Anna!"

"Let's hope it's a girl instead." I was playing along, but I wasn't sure at all. Like Marco, I too dreamed of starting a family before I got too old; the image came from the ads, with Dad, Mom and two seemingly perfect children. It was all fine as long as it was a fantasy; in reality, I didn't want a child. Not yet. I lacked the urge, the true desire. I had time. Right now I had a husband who I loved and who loved me and a good life with everything I wanted.

Marco got up and planted a kiss on my forehead. "Luckily, we have a big enough house, with the extra room." In that room and in the living room, too, we would put up friends from Italy who came to visit us. Marco looked around in satisfaction, then he kept going on as I was clearing the table. I was laughing to myself in the kitchen as he carried on from the bathroom, even while he was brushing his teeth.

We were almost late for work. We put on our overcoats and a few minutes later we were trotting along the street, heading for the subway. It was a gray day, with drizzle. Now I was feeling unhappy. Marco's good humor had not rubbed off on me completely, as it did almost every day. I felt conflicted, irritated by the idea that all I was left with was a choice conditioned by my being a woman and a wife. I remember that I turned around to look at him: he was smiling at the rain. That same smile he gave me every morning as soon as he woke up was one of the reasons I had fallen in love with him.

"Well, Anna, shall we give it a try?" He was off again. He was overdoing it, yet Marco usually tackled any problem with the right measure.

"Try what?" I replied, sulkily. I was seated in the packed subway car while he stood in front of me. In a minute we would arrive at his stop, Bryant Park, while I would go on a little farther.

"The baby. Our baby," he snorted.

"Look, this is your stop." I gave him a gentle punch in the stomach. I was annoyed because he hadn't noticed my reaction and also because, just for once, our wishes did not coincide. I had discovered something beyond the perfection that was our love, and I perceived it as a threat.

In the meantime, he had moved away and was heading for the platform; "Ciao!" he almost shouted to attract my gaze. I returned that with a nod that lacked any warmth. In the handful of seconds before the train moved off, Marco was almost half way up the steps leading to the exit; from above he could catch a glimpse of me and every day he would say goodbye with a smile. Two signs of understanding that fit like a jigsaw as long as our eyes remained in contact. Our secret ritual. A gesture that would stay with us until evening.

That day, for the first time, I didn't respond. I pretended I was looking at my watch.

I knew I could be independent in every way, if need be. That's what I told myself.

A few weeks went by and he didn't bring up the subject again. There had been no way to because we had an Italian friend as a houseguest. Our house was a port of call, open to all our friends who came to visit us and even strangers or friends of friends who arrived in New York looking for a job. We put them up on the Ikea sofa bed; the welcome was a way of satisfying our need to repay the good fortune we had enjoyed.

That time it was Gabriele; he was from Rome and wanted to be a director. "My girlfriend is pregnant." It was confession time, he was leaving for California the next day and perhaps we would never meet again.

"Congratulations! When are you getting married?" I asked indiscreetly as I served coffee; I had cooked an Italian meal especially for him.

"I asked her." Gabriele looked at the floor sheepishly while he stroked his beard. "Not only did she turn me down, she also told me she wouldn't keep the baby. She didn't want it." A moment of embarrassment followed, in which each of us busied ourselves stirring sugar into the scalding liquid. Marco's eyes were narrowed and he seemed impassive; instead, he was disgusted. I knew him too well to see that. I was amazed, I didn't understand. "Why? If you love each other..."

"She's a bitch, an egotist. She and her freedom come first. How did she put it? 'I have to think of my career, just as you do.' Do you see? She'd rather be a theater actress!" Gabriele stared at Marco, then at me, twirling the pack of cigarettes in his hand because he wasn't allowed to smoke in the house.

"How come you got yourselves into this situation?" Marco was pragmatic even when love was involved.

"It must have been chance. These things happen," I had replied, instinctively. An automatic defense that wasn't really necessary.

"Exactly. One spring night, after an evening with friends, we ended the day in grand style and, just for once, we weren't careful. Once is enough for always. I had already asked her to marry me."

"And she got cold feet." Marco, paying very close attention, summed the story up, his gaze trained rather intrusively on his friend.

"Actually, she never said yes." Gabriele got up to go to the window. The lights in the surrounding buildings offered glimpses of family life. On a closer look it was evident that almost all the women were busy with something.

"If she wasn't sure, she was right to choose in an honest way." I picked up the tray with the coffee cups, now empty. Now I, too, was one of the busy women, a part of the view for anyone looking out of their window.

"She aborted my child." Gabriele was on the verge of tears, his chin trembling. I left them alone, him and Marco. Let them sort it out between men. I didn't know what to think about that woman who had done something I didn't agree with. Yet it didn't seem right to condemn her without appeal. She must have had her reasons and, besides, goodness knows what's it like in Italy for an unmarried mother.

I went into the bathroom, where I found a stain—my period had arrived. I was young, in love, with a job, friends and a house. I lived in New York, I traveled and, well, I had no hindrances. Children are fine when they come along at the right time. We would have them when the time was right.

One thing at a time.

I wanted to choose, and I could choose. I felt that my life was up to me. Through the door I heard Marco's voice; maybe he was trying to console Gabriele, maybe he was preaching a bit. Sometimes I thought Marco was too sure of himself, that he wanted to decide for me too; he would put me to the test by showing me the path, then wait to see which way I went. This business of the baby, for example. He would start pushing again while I backpedaled. I liked the idea, too, but I was in no hurry. It seemed like a great thing and a massive hassle at the same time. It would be a game to be played between Marco and me. Or just between me and myself. There would be no winner, or perhaps we would all win. In the end, even the idea of being able to choose was a fraud, or better yet, an illusion.

My mother had never known that there was another possibility. In her day you got married to have children, you worked to live and you pretended to be content with the life you led. If somebody was truly happy, that was a blessing, especially down my way.

Marco's mother, Cristina, had had the same fate, too. You just had to look at that photo he was so fond of—the sad eyes that reflected piles of laundry to be washed, homework assignments to be checked—monotonous days that saw her dead tired by evening, without even the desire to dream. A maelstrom of despondency.

Another epoch. It would be different for me.

Children when the time was right.

But when? Now that Marco didn't want kids anymore.

# 2
# LIFE IS MY PROFESSION

When I was small my mother used to take me to the cemetery every Saturday afternoon, unless it was too cold or pouring rain. In those cases she would say, "Not today. Grandmother says not to go, anyway she's got her friends to keep her company." So I would stay home to color my drawing book, gluing trading cards into it and pestering my brother to play with me. In first grade, by Christmas I had already learned to read and write. The next time I went back to the cemetery I read the words over the entrance, "We were like you, you will be like us." I was sure that the words belonged to the cemetery in my town, but later I found them in other graveyards, even far away from there. Every time I noticed the inscription I felt perturbed. It seemed that in those places all that existed was the past and the future; the passing of the baton between the life that had been and death left no space for the present, which was never spoken of, considered only the harbinger of a catastrophe located in some indeterminate, undefined time in the making. Yet I was in the present every time I came across those words engraved above a gate, maybe on a bend on a country road or in the outskirts of a city I had chanced to visit.

Even now I feel that way: in the making.

I don't know if I should try to have this baby. Together we could construct the future. A future only with him.

"Ask Marco. What does Marco say about it? But is Marco okay with it? Marco's right! You're a goose!" My mother's words echo in my head, she who had also been a mother to Marco and who always sided with him, the man, the husband, the son-in-law, in any case, the *boss*. Every so often, laughing, I would throw that in her face and she would give me a serious look and say in her dialect: "Get on with you, girl. You must listen to your man. Understand?"

When Marco came into the family I took second place. I had discovered, to this day and despite all the fine words, that down my way, the roles of daughter and mother are inferior to the positions of the son and son-in-law.

Yet I had more life experience under my belt than my parents did. Born and raised in Camponogara, I went to small schools in the outskirts, and I dreamed of traveling the world and I had already done that by high school; then there had been the Erasmus project in Germany, university in Venice, lots of trips to many countries. I put myself out there, with my own efforts, and I had found my fortune in New York. Not only that, I had also obtained citizenship.

I am from the Veneto, or rather, as Marco puts it, I'm a Venetian who has conquered New York.

The Veneto is a world in itself, full of sweet, modulated sounds; it's mostly flatland, with few hills and few mountains. I have kept up the traditions of my compatriots—the Venetians have always been great travelers, good at business, and curious about the world.

Even when I was small I would sniff the wind that brought the smell of the sea. I liked to imagine how far it might go rolling and whistling as it hugged the curve of the Earth, while it blended with other odors, ambassadors of lands to be explored. I was proud of my origins, but I knew that one day I would leave everything behind and go far away. I would leave, alone, and I would make my discoveries. Effort and sacrifice have never scared me and now I earn enough to permit myself a few little luxuries; to use an expression dear to Marco, I help keep the wheels of the economy turning much more than a lot of men.

I'm a New Yorker now, or maybe I am to the same extent that I have remained a Venetian.

My mother doesn't understand this, she finds it hard to accept having such an independent daughter. When we talk on Skype, her voice is always heavy with anxiety, "How are you, all alone there?" She can never resist asking that question, an implied wish that I might return to Italy.

"I'm good, Mom. I get by just fine, don't worry." In reality I'm trying to be alone. When I go out for a walk I'm no longer sure where I should go. New York is full of places that were special for Marco and me, and I keep going back to them, even though it hurts.

Perhaps it would be different if I lived my new life with our son?

What would life be like with a child? Complicated. Here no one makes it easy for you, but if you get your act together you can make it. I am a list person, I try to evaluate priorities, to draw up lists in which important commitments and trivial errands fit into place perfectly. I can do that even with a child.

If there is a problem, you just find the solution. Marco taught me that. It's a method that works, almost always.

I read somewhere that it's hard at first to get used to solitude, and then being alone becomes a vice: withdrawing from life, shutting yourself off from social contacts, cultivating rituals and private habits and constructing your own world inside a bubble that no one can penetrate. My feet always take me to the places where I hope to meet Marco: our bench in Bryant Park, our favorite table at Max SoHa, or the one on the second floor of the Met where, depending on the time, the light plays over the Tiffany windows.

For me it's one step forward and two steps back. I never reach my destination. My point of arrival, and new departure, might be the baby.

I wonder, in my situation, whether the baby and I would be truly alone. A sweet isolation, that of mother and child. Would it be like that?

I'd like to ask Marco.

I must clean house in my head. Make order, draw up a list. Discard and dump the garbage, the mistaken ideas, the things others push me to do, the routine that no longer belongs to me.

To air my thoughts, that's what I need to do.

If Marco were at my side now, he'd say, "Yes, do that. Drop everything and start again. Start over!"

I turn the corner and come across the joyful barking of Yepa, the basset hound I occasionally meet near my place. Her owner smiles at me, tugs at the leash and calls her. The bow-wowing has woken me up. I realize that I'm on my street and I don't know how I got there. These days I often run on autopilot and go where my legs take me. This is not good. I am losing chunks of life: minutes, hours, half days, and it's a waste.

"You must always be aware of what you're doing. At the worst get rid of the superfluous things, drop the useless ones, but pay attention to all the rest." Marco's voice echoes in my head, and he's right. This way life has more flavor, like a morning kiss given in haste because the alarm didn't go off.

It would happen from time to time. I would be in a rush, but all the same, I would notice the slightly salty flavor of his skin, the warm odor of the night, the sheets rumpled by love. I would hit the shower and immediately let out a screech at the first jet of icy water, a habit he–who felt the cold–had never shared. Ah, Marco, who was impeccably dressed by day and lounged around in ridiculous outfits in the intimacy of home in the evening, especially during the cold time of year. I had never managed to make him change his habits.

"I get it from my mom," he said as he put on heavy pajama pants, pulling them up almost to his armpits. "When I was small, Cristina used to make me wear long johns made of this real coarse wool, but they were warm." In the meantime, he was fiddling with some thick socks into which he stuck the legs of his pajama bottoms. I was laughing as he carried on explaining that back in the day his long johns were a kind of hugely uncomfortable armor; they irritated his skin, but had the merit of making him feel secure.

"I'll keep you warm, my prince," I said.

"How? You're too thin, and cold, too. You sleep naked! Let's be clear, it's not that I don't like that..." And as he watched me getting undressed, he stuck his top inside his pants. He looked as if enclosed in an impenetrable cocoon. Every evening after he got dressed and after a few moments of silence, he would turn toward me and stretch out his hand over the sheet, waggling his index and middle fingers in imitation of two legs walking. He took my hand, caressed it, and held it tight. I would pretend to be asleep.

"Anna?" he would whisper, then persisted, "Anna! How was your day?" Then I would give in and start to tell him about even the silly things, the banter in the office, and he would do the same. Our talks often included plans for the future: careers and travel, too, special vacations for just us–either alone or with some Italian friends. And then...later on it always ended with the last kiss, "Goodnight, Princess," he used to say to me.

I push open the door of my building. A rectangular package is protruding from the mailbox. How wonderful! I know what's in it; I was expecting it.

Since I've been living alone I sometimes have wishes that must be granted instantly. At times they are small things of no value, except for me, and I itch to get my hands on whatever it is that interests me; it becomes a fixation that I focus on without allowing myself any distractions. A way of forgetting that Marco is no longer with me.

Even before the elevator doors have closed behind me I'm already tearing away at the thin cardboard. I feel the dark red cover of the Italian edition of *The House of the Spirits* and I run my fingertip over the outline of the balcony depicted in the middle of the cover. I enter my dark and desolate apartment, and I get the impression that a slight current of air is flowing across the living room.

Isabel Allende! Chile! Still standing, my bag still slung over my shoulder, I open the book and read a phrase, "Just as when we come into the world, when we die we are afraid of the unknown. But the fear is something from within us that has nothing to do with reality. Dying is like being born: merely a change."

I'd like to cry, but I resist. Marco used to say, "Direct your thoughts at something you like."

I take a piece of fruit from the basket on the table, a lovely red apple, and I see the Atacama Desert once more; I'd like to be there, in the Valley of the Moon. I bite into the apple—it has no flavor, but my desire to travel had lots of that. At sixteen I had already persuaded my folks to let me go to Chile for a short course promoted by the school. In those days I loved Neruda and Allende. I had just read *The House of the Spirits* and I had seen the movie with Meryl Streep and Antonio Banderas. A phrase had stuck in my head, "life is my profession," and it became my mantra. That was where my journey began; Chile was to be my first destination. I stayed in South America for six months, enough time to change me inside and out. I came back home with my hair dyed blonde, carrying an extra twenty pounds thanks to too many cakes, and the oddity, in those days at least, of a small tattoo—a butterfly in a place my mother would have defined as embarrassing. I had also embraced the idea, more than the substance, of a first love with a local guy, Rodrigo. Telling this story to Marco condemned me to endless teasing. The name Rodrigo prompted him to make all kinds of wisecracks; it became a catchphrase and I would usually laugh it off, but when I was in a bad mood it irritated me. I wonder what Rodrigo looks like today? I'm thirty-three now, he's thirty-four.

Marco's thirty-six, come to that.

Anyway, I had a huge crush on Rodrigo and when I got home I began writing him, but he soon stopped replying to my letters. The final blow came from one of my Chilean girlfriends—Rodrigo was dating another girl. It didn't matter and it didn't even count that he didn't keep in touch anymore. I was sure, if we got together again, that everything would have been like before and all I thought about was when I could go back there. I would have to prepare the ground for my parents' inevitable opposition. One argument in my favor would have been having at least a part of the money needed for the journey. At the end of the school year, I had looked for a summer job; the right break came with a three-star hotel in Venice that was looking for a part-time concierge. People from all over the world arrived at my desk; I checked the bookings, recommended the best restaurants to the clients, and gave them suggestions for unusual itineraries through the most evocative and lesser-known parts of the city.

I take a chunk of Parmesan from the fridge and the already open bottle of prosecco. I grab a plate and a cheese knife and put everything on a tray. I add a pack of thick bread sticks and a napkin, actually two of them—I don't want to mark the book I care so much about. I sit down on the couch, drink a sip of wine, and eat. The book is beside me; I smile at the cover and look forward to the moment when I can bury myself in it. Inside there are the words that, many years ago, put me on the road that led me here. To Marco.

# 3
## TAKE A RUN UP

The hotel I was slaving in in Venice would be my gateway to the world. In order to win the right to travel, I put my heart and soul into my work. I dispensed smiles and advice to the tourists while I sniffed the faint odor of the places they came from and to which I dreamed of going, one day. With the foreigners I had the chance to improve my English and German, and to brush up the Spanish I had learned so well. I went to work by train and, if I met no one to have a little chat with, I practiced thinking in one of the languages I knew.

I wanted to be ready to leave.

Every so often I was on shift during the weekends, too. That September Sunday I was coming back from Venice and the train was racing along beneath a layer of big gray clouds whose edges shaded into titanium. I usually went home from the station on my bicycle, but that day my father was waiting for me. He had called me mid-morning to let me know: the sky threatened something more than a shower, but with the car, we would get home in ten minutes or so. We'd have lunch all together and on time, for a change.

"How did it go, kiddo?" Dad stretched across the seat to open my door. "Where's the bicycle, so we can load it up?" The scent of the Little Trees pine air freshener was swamped by the Italian hair spray he used liberally, so much so that his hair was stiff as a board.

"I'll go get it. It's tied up over there." I pointed to the pole in front of the patisserie, on the sidewalk across the way. "Shall we pick up some pastries?"

He gave me a sidelong look, arousing my guilty feelings about the extra pounds I had gained during my stay in Chile, some of which I still had to lose. My family was determined to get me back in shape with a diet that was way too strict for me.

"Mom has already seen to that." He added a few words that died away as he moved to get out of the car.

"Only fruit for me?" I smiled, and as I was shutting the door I saw he was about to cross the street.

"Leave it, Dad! I'll go, it's padlocked. You open the trunk." As I unchained the bicycle, out of the corner of my eye I reviewed the cakes in the window and filled my lungs with their irresistible aroma.

"What are you doing here?" Bea, my best friend since high school days, had just come out of the store with a tray of pastries balanced on the palm of her hand.

"What are *you* doing here? I'm on my way home." I nodded toward my father, on the other side of the street.

"I'm going to lunch with my sister," she replied, making the tray teeter. "Are those pants new? You got them a size too small." She gave a sour snicker.

"They're not new. They're from before I went to Chile." I grabbed the handlebar of the bicycle with both hands. I was gripping it so hard my knuckles were white.

Bea wore a condescending smirk; things had always been that way between us, even at school. She always won.

"Oh, pants from when you were thiiin..." Now she was mocking me openly. "You'll see, sooner or later you'll lose a few pounds, that way you'll find a boyfriend and then you'll get pregnant and you'll get fat and you won't lose weight anymore between one baby and the next."

"No. I'm going to travel the world. I don't want to settle for second-best," I replied without looking at her. Since my return I had been less easy on Bea. I was no longer the little girl who always gave in to her. I had flown away and had already seen some of the world while she had only gone as far as Venice, at most.

"Do you want a ride, Bea?" My father pointed to the big clouds scudding across the sky. "Where are you headed? You don't even have an umbrella," he yelled to make himself heard from where he was.

"Thanks. It doesn't matter. My sister lives at the end of the street." She smiled and I noticed the chipped incisor, the result of a nasty fall from her scooter a year before. It was a worry for Bea, because she ought to get it fixed, but she was terrified of the dentist.

"Well, haven't you decided to get that tooth fixed yet? What does it take? Okay, nobody's perfect." My attack came to nothing, and her smile remained in place. She was a tough nut and had even strengthened her defenses since her boyfriend had dumped her. The one she thought she would marry. She had become a very young old maid, envious of all her girl friends who had not yet been disappointed by life. She was especially nasty to girls like me, who had plans and a better chance of a different future. I should have stopped considering her my best friend; I realized that all she wanted was to push me around and that deep down she was jealous of my traveling, and the ease with which I learned languages. Every day the gulf between us grew deeper, but I was fond of her and that was why I put up with her rudeness.

Seeing her there in front of me with her broken tooth and an uncertain grin on her face, I felt a surge of affection. "Bye, Bea!" She wasn't expecting my hug and the tray of pastries almost wound up on the ground.

"Have a nice Sunday and say hi to your sister."

"Yes, thanks. Say hi to your mom, too." She grasped the package with both hands, then she yelled: "See you, Mr. Venier! Have a nice day." He nodded in response.

"Peace is made," I thought. "At least until the next spat." I turned away from Bea and went back across the road carrying my bicycle, happy to get back to the dirty air of the station, away from temptation. If Dad hadn't come to pick me up, I would have had a cream puff as an appetizer.

"About time you got moving. Always chatting with Bea, and I'll bet that tonight you'll both be on the phone for at least three hours," he grumbled as he made room in the trunk. I helped him by taking one wheel; in the end we managed to get the frame and handlebars inside and closed the trunk.

"My hands are filthy!" I looked in my bag for something to clean myself with while Dad got back in the driver's seat.

"I'm starving!" I added, as I got into the seat.

"So, let's go!" the ticking of the blinker signaled our exit from the parking lot. "Now we're late. Risotto with radicchio and sausage is waiting for us. Your brother will already be there with fork in hand."

"Ah, risotto! Will you give me a spoonful, too? Come on, Dad, let's make it quick!" He hit the gas and in a moment the Alfa Romeo was through the yellow light. Another blip on the pedal and we were in the middle of the intersection at the same moment in which a truck was going up through the gears to cross it. It had gotten the green light.

The impact was very loud and our car started spinning like a top. The truck hit the passenger side and my father, although hurt, came off better than I did. After they got me to the hospital I was in a coma for twenty days. I had broken both of my hip bones, my right femur, my left ankle , and I also had some internal injuries. In order to get back on my feet, I had to undergo several surgeries and it was almost a year before I could walk again.

"Hi, Anna. Take it easy, everything's okay." When I woke up in the hospital I saw a man with a beard and white lab coat. "You had an accident in the car with your dad. He's fine." As he talked he listened to my heart. "How do you feel?"

"Fine," I muttered, trying to understand where I was. "I don't remember..." I started to get agitated, moving my hands and trying to grab the bars at the side of the bed.

"Stop! Don't move." In the end they immobilized my hands for the whole time I was under morphine.

The months of convalescence spent in enforced inactivity proved to be a turning point.

I was eighteen and as far as my family was concerned, my path was already laid out: to go ahead with my course in Mediterranean languages and culture and then a job, an inevitable encounter with a local guy, and a *normal* life. Perhaps, before the accident, Mom and Dad would have succeeded in curbing my life, leading me in the direction they wanted, persuading me to give up on traveling, but now my dreams were greater than that.

Confined to bed, immobile, and obliged to be cared for, I still found a way to escape the prison of the hospital. I remembered the words of my Italian teacher in junior high; she had taught us that studying, being informed, and reading books and newspapers were fundamental, the indispensable basis for thinking and forming an opinion on events.

The best solution was surfing the net. With the Internet I could go anywhere, learn new things, even meet new friends. In the meantime, I had begun to get better and I had gone from the bed to a wheelchair, then to crutches, first two and then one and, finally, after a long period of rehabilitation, I was walking once more.

I decided to change my university course and enrolled in Foreign Business Studies, a faculty that called for the study of three foreign languages and would help me find a job. Moreover, it offered a chance to access internships, the most interesting of which was with Valentino in New York. I also took advantage of the Erasmus program to spend a year in Germany.

I wanted to see the world in order to know other cultures and also to try my luck. I had decided to bet on myself and I wanted to win.

I was pulsing with passion and enthusiasm.

I felt strong even though I hadn't used my legs for too long. But once I took the run up I didn't stop until five years later, after my arrival in New York.

# 4
# THE FIRST LEVEL OF PARADISE

*New York, Friday, May 26, 2006*
That time during the landing I hadn't closed my eyes as I usually do. The view had captivated me, making me almost forget my fear. New York shimmered on a fantastic sunny day. The airport contained everything in one spot. The space, every little space, was occupied by an infinite assortment of humanity drawn by the hand of some visionary painter. I managed to retrieve my suitcase fairly quickly. At the terminal there was a jumble of cabs, buses, shuttles and limos, all waiting.

I knew how to find my way because I had made a careful study of the route before leaving. I headed for the Airtrain, the elevated train that runs from JFK to Jamaica Station and from there, with the subway, to Manhattan, Queens and the Bronx. Covering the entire route took me over an hour. I was exhausted, the tiredness mixed with anxiety. I had an appointment with the Turkish girl whose apartment I was going to share. All I knew about her was what Federico had told me; he was the mutual friend who knew her from his time in New York, about a year before. Federico had put us in touch and Asena and I had exchanged a few e-mails to agree on the rent and the date of my arrival. But what if she let me down for some reason?

I took the yellow subway line and got off at Elmhurst Avenue, in Queens, then I went up to the street dragging my suitcase behind me. At the top of the steps I got my breath back and noticed a girl whose face wore a hesitant look; she was wearing small round glasses and a light jumpsuit, gray with pink edging. She was waving a card with my name on it.

I waved and she smiled. I ran to hug her with my suitcase bouncing along behind me.

"Anna, you're Anna. You look so elegant!" she exclaimed as she detached herself from my embrace. In reality I was hot, dusty and creased.

"You must be tired!" She gestured at me to follow her. I touched her arm to get her attention and she eyed me curiously.

"Asena?" I asked, suddenly suspicious.

"Yes," she replied. "Who did you think I was?" She laughed in a funny way, drawing the air in from her mouth.

"Federico says hello," I said, reassured.

We walked up the street at a steady pace. Asena pointed out things that might be useful to me. I didn't pay much attention to her, intent as I was in studying the faces of the people, the many different ethnic groups, and the peeling wooden houses. We slowed down in front of a store that sold a bit of everything. A Chinese man was standing in the doorway, a cigarette in one hand and a can of Coke in the other. A Chihuahua was curled up at his feet. The man smiled at Asena, who smiled back and bent down to pat the dog, which got up and took a few steps, wagging its tail: it was lame. I had just enough time to glimpse a big poster of Che Guevara through the window.

"What kind of place is this?" I asked.

"It's our local deli. It'll be the saving of your lunches and dinners, you'll see. The Chinese people who run it always keep it open, even at night. Doggy is their guard dog," she concluded with a laugh.

We went on. The sparse trees that lined the street seemed in poor shape, yet for me everything was magnificent. In that moment Asena took my arm. "Right, we're here. This is our house and look..." she stretched out an arm. "That's Queens Library right there." She succeeded in shaking me out of my torpor. I looked around. If my mother had known what kind of place I had ended up in she would have felt ill. For me it was the beginning of a new life; I felt I would be just fine there.

I wasn't able to memorize every detail of my new home straight off, but later it all became familiar to me. We crossed a small yard before going up the few steps that led to the rundown door of an old building. It was red, with peeling paint, and the windows were part white and part brown. Some of the façade was brick, while the plasterwork began on the second floor. On the left there was a fire escape, just like the ones you see in the movies; to the other side another stairway led down one floor toward an entry over which the insignia of the Methodist Church was clearly visible.

We went in, welcomed by the smell of cabbage and piss mixed with the muffled yelling of an argument that was going on behind the door of the first-floor apartment. I wrinkled my nose just as Asena turned toward me.

"Disappointed? Were you expecting better?" she asked, a little coolly.

"No, of course not!" I replied. "It's just that I like cabbage but I can't stomach pee." It wasn't much of a gag and maybe it didn't even make sense, translated into my English, but she started to laugh, a bit out of sync, after me. In the end we had understood each other. I followed her up two flights of stairs that once must have had some pretensions to elegance. The wallpaper, partly unstuck, was decorated with lines of stylized camels against a mint-colored background; the wine-red carpeting continued all the way to the door of the apartment I was going to share with Asena. In the living room, the turquoise of the walls clashed with the tiled floor and its arabesque pattern; there was a big couch in burnt brown leather with sagging cushions while the round tables of various sizes scattered around the room were cluttered with books, candles and succulents—cactus and echeveria.

"This is your room." Asena threw open the door and gave me a hesitant look. "The girl who left took away the extra stuff, I'm sorry." There was only a bed, not even a bedside table.

"It's okay. I'll think about it later. Now all I need is a chair to put my clothes on." We were facing one another, and I stretched out my hands and took hers. Asena returned the gesture and all embarrassment was overcome.

"Does your name have a meaning?" I asked.

"Asena is the name of the she-wolf who, according to our tradition, brought forth the Turkish people. Maybe I'll tell you the story once you've rested."

I wanted to chat, take a look around and, at the same time, I was flagging; I was so tired that I had to make a real effort to resist sleep. My new friend noticed this. She didn't ask any questions, but offered me some chocolate muffins and a Turkish coffee, then she suggested I lie down on the bed.

I woke up the following morning, a Saturday that was as bright as a floodlight. Still sleepy, I followed the sound of the radio coming from the living room. Asena was shuffling a deck of cards as she sipped her coffee.

"Hi! Cut the deck and help yourself," she said as she pushed the cards and a cup toward me. I obeyed without thinking, breathing in the aroma of coffee. She took back the cards and stared at me, seriously. "It's fresh from the machine, I made it in your honor. Of course, it won't be like the espresso you make in Italy..."

"Let me taste it. I bet it's great." I was critically jet lagged. I discovered immediately that the coffee was disgusting, but I gave Asena a grateful look.

"I know that you're jet lagged. Try to get back on track. The sooner you do, the better. I've been through it many times."

"Thanks, Asena. Do you like solitaire?"

She looked at me in amazement and burst out laughing: "Hey, I'm reading your cards, you know."

"You are? Why?"

"I always do it when I meet someone I have to have dealings with, and you and I will be sharing the house for a while. Trust me. In the meantime, why not take a look around?"

I didn't wait to be asked twice, but I wasn't happy about the business with the cards. Superstition didn't come into it. I had never believed in fortune-tellers and the tarot. I went into the tiny kitchen, a niche in the wall more than anything else; the equipment was made up of an electric stove, a microwave oven and a dilapidated fridge, as well as four shelves.

I went into the bathroom, leaving the door open. There was no bidet, and when I arrived I had been in such a whirl that I hadn't noticed. Luckily there was a shower instead of a tub. I noticed that Asena's supply of creams and makeup was very spartan. There was no trace of lipstick and not even perfume. I returned to the living room, stretching as I went. The aroma of coffee still lingered in the air and that was a consolation.

"Where did you learn to read cards?" I asked. From above us there came the sound of something falling over, followed by a resounding *fuck*.

"A friend at university taught me," Asena replied, holding a card in midair.

"The faculty of astrology?" I twisted my mouth in a laugh that was also a yawn.

"Yes. The lecturer is a friend of mine. Do you know that..." She was drumming the table with the fingers of her left hand while she constantly stroked a card between the fingers of her right.

"What?"

"Take a look around while you're here. There will be an unmissable opportunity."

"A job? Will it go well? Will they hire me?"

"Better than that! By any chance did you break things off with a guy back in Italy? You're going to meet someone here."

"Sure," I laughed, but she had grown serious. "He'll be the love of my life. We'll get married and live happily ever after." I set the empty cup down on the table and spun around. "Is that it?"

"More or less. I have to go now." She picked up the cards and, despite my insistence, I couldn't get her to say anything more. I had things to do, too. I had planned to check out the office that, starting the following Monday, would be my place of work for the next three months. In fact, when I had written to ask if I might show up at the office already on the Saturday they had immediately said I could. I sorted out my things, taking out my clothes and laying them on the chair. The rest I left in the suitcase. I was in a hurry.

Before taking a shower, I turned the dial of the radio looking for goodness knows what. I stopped on the notes of

*Promiscuous*. I didn't like the Nelly Furtado song, but it was familiar and that was enough for me. Moving to the syncopated rhythm of that piece, I laid out on the bed the suit I was going to wear: white shorts above the knee and a sailor T-shirt with white and gray stripes, and pumps with pointed toes. I called them my *Minnie shoes*, and they were among my favorites; in fact, I was downright proud of them. The outfit was casual, besides, it was Saturday morning and mine would only be a courtesy visit, just to have a look around. Inside I was trembling. I wanted to make a good impression and hoped my coworkers would be friendly. I figured that here in New York, everyone took their work very seriously. That was nothing new to me, where I come from it was the same. New Yorkers would certainly have a lot to teach me and I couldn't wait to learn, to fit in. To feel, here in New York as if I was at home.

I left very early for the appointment because I knew that Manhattan was pretty far from the part of Queens I was in. I did fairly well. I took the subway to Manhattan and got off at Times Square instead of Bryant Park, because I wanted to soak up the atmosphere of the city. Times Square was only one block from 42nd Street, where my future office was, but when I arrived there I got lost. I couldn't find the building. I started walking backward and forward along the same stretch of sidewalk without managing to spot number eleven, which was my destination. I decided to ask a passerby and discovered that the sign with the number I was looking for was placed just inside the entry, a bit hidden. The building had an austere look; in the lobby, which was clad in smoky white and hazel marble, I was greeted by the doorman. I showed my document to have permission to go up, and I got a visitor's pass.

"Twenty-sixth floor," the man said and he pointed to the elevators.

It was my ascent to paradise. The doors opened onto white: a marble floor and walls on which the enormous Valentino sign stood out in gold lettering. Beside this hung the works of famous photographers who had immortalized some of the models who had made history. On the floor there was a large red carpet. There were also various couches in white leather and the front desk, which was deserted on a Saturday. Almost immediately the door that led into the heart of the offices opened.

"Anna Venier?" A man with a cordial smile held the door open and moved to one side. "Rosario Montrone," he introduced himself, ushering me in. "Did you have a good trip? Have you settled in?" His handshake was vigorous and his deep voice matched his solid physique. His jacket, the color of a blushing salmon, made me smile, it was discordant but fun.

"Yes, thanks." I followed him into the maze of corridors while I peeked through the open doors of some offices.

At the end of the corridor he turned toward me. "We're all on first name terms here. There are lots of nice people, you'll see. Here, this is my office." I stopped in the doorway, enchanted by the huge windows looking out over Bryant Park. With one look I could take in the Empire State Building, which I recognized immediately, the New York Public Library and, in the distance, all of Downtown, places that would become familiar very soon. Everything was enormous, outsized, apart from the people who, at the bottom of the precipice of the skyscraper, trailed along like a colony of ants.

"Anna? Your name is Anna, right?" a voice asked from outside my field of vision.

"Anna Venier."

"Rosario, the girl is in shock." A cordial laugh came from behind me. I didn't turn around; I was hypnotized by the view.

"It always has this effect, the first time," Rosario said. "Of course, they're the tallest skyscrapers in the world."

"Down there in back, is that the place where they put the skating rink for Christmas?" I asked in a low voice.

"The girl likes to skate!" said the voice from before. This time I turned around.

"I thought I'd never get your attention. Marco Falcioni." He shook my hand with both of his. "I'm from Fano, in the Marche, Rosario is Sicilian and our boss is from Voghera.[1] You're among friends. Welcome to New York's own slice of Italy!" Marco was wearing a Smurf-colored polo shirt. His smile and his manner were as welcoming as a hug.

I was struck by the difference between the two men: Rosario, tall and solidly built, and Marco, tall and rangy.

"I'm sorry," I said, my gaze returning to the outside. "I can't believe I'm here. This view is incredible."

"It's the heart of Midtown. You'll get used to it."

Rosario had subsided into the executive chair with his back turned to the sight on the other side of the window. "You'll take the tour of wonders, too. We've all gone through it."

He looked up and stared at me for a few seconds. "You won't manage to see very much of the city in three months. The whole world is here and it's impossible to get bored. But if you know how to look, you'll find your El Dorado. Every one of us finds something for him or herself."

"I wonder what our Anna will find!" Marco had drawn up an armchair and put it in a spot from where I could carry on looking outside, with the feeling of floating on air. He touched my arm to invite me to take a seat.

"A chain of skyscrapers," I said as I sat down without losing visual contact with the outside.

"And that would be?" Marco said.

"The mountain chain of New York" I replied.

"We've got a poet here." Rosario was amused. "You know you'll be dealing with numbers, don't you? By the way, I won't be your boss. You'll meet Jeff Kaminski on Monday."

"I'd like to see where I'll be working. Is that possible?" I had recovered. Now I was observing the rest of the office. As well as Montrone's desk, there was another, more modest one set to one side. Marco was sitting there. In order to take part in the conversation he had turned his chair around and had his back to the monitor of his PC. I thought it must be awkward to work with your boss checking you out from behind. No way to surf for personal reasons, no game of solitaire for an unplanned break, hard to send a private e-mail too, with him present.

"Of course," Montrone said. "Marco, would you mind accompanying Anna? I'll make a call and I'll join you in the kitchen for coffee."

I went straight to the office door and peered out into the corridor, followed by Marco. He gripped my elbow lightly, to steer me. I gave him a surreptitious look: I had forgotten his last name.

# 5
## WHAT DO WOMEN WANT?

*New York, June 2006*

I liked everything about New York: my job, the way I felt free in the midst of a sea of people, each with their own destination. In the mornings, riding the packed subway, I was a mere dot in the universe, yet I knew I counted for something. I had my place, my mission; I was going in a precise direction and leading my life.

I could choose. I had already done that by leaving Italy, and I would do it again other times. I would adapt and I would always move ahead. Printed on my forehead, in invisible letters, was the motto 'The world is my home.'

In the office I learned new things about the job and about the people I met. I had begun to understand that I had to be discreet with everyone and that I could relax only with Italians, without having to worry too much about curbing my natural exuberance. An exuberance that was, ultimately, the enthusiasm I felt for having arrived in New York.

I was discovering an aspect of the American spirit. If you apply yourself and show your worth, then others will help you, open things up for you, and have faith in you. Nobody cares who you are and where you come from. If you know what you're doing, if you work well, then you move forward. I filtered whatever I saw or heard through a benign judgment, a kind of blindness that always made me feel charged up, happy, full of energy and hope. It was the drive of youth. I was lucky, sure, but the chance of an internship with Valentino was the fruit of my own efforts and not of connections, as was the case with many Italians, spoiled rich kids related to god knows whom.

I felt strong, very strong.

Every so often I was seized by a certain wistfulness, a longing for my family, friends, and home, but it would pass in a flash. Besides, I was going to stay in New York for only three months, then I would decide which other path to take.

I was living in a state of exultation. For me every day was a new beginning, a rebirth. I had to learn everything over in the same way as I had to learn to walk again after the accident. Here the goal was to get the hang of shopping, eating, getting around the city, managing relations with people...living. Everything!

Working in a fashion house means respecting some basic rules. At Valentino my job was in accounts, yet I was obliged, as was everyone, to ensure that my outfits were in line with the house style, which required you to dress soberly in only four basic colors: white, gray, blue and black, and the various shades thereof. It was permitted to wear colorful clothes too, provided they were made by Valentino. As employees we had a bonus to spend on the *maison's* clothes and we also had access to some particularly advantageous discount offers, but for my pockets, the prices were still prohibitive. Another indispensable requisite was to be slim enough to wear the famous size four. That at least was not a problem, because I was slim again even though I ate anything, and plenty of it.

I was twenty-two and I had a job I liked, one in which I wanted to give my best. The first days were frantic, I was afraid I wasn't quick enough in responding to the requests that landed on my table. My colleagues were all kind, competent, and willing to help, even though they were very busy, yet I was terrified of making mistakes, of being reprimanded; for this reason I checked everything twice, always trying to do well and do it quick. There was always a good deal of work and many people worked late, depending on deadlines. On the other hand, I got to meet lots of new friends: Italians, Americans and other nationalities. Speaking three languages, as well as my own, was an advantage. I realized that every day was going to be a party full of surprises.

"So, tomorrow evening you're coming out with us." Fabrizio was one of my Italian colleagues and also a friend of Marco's. He was from Fano, too. Like me he was an intern, and all three of us had met several times, during coffee breaks.

"I'm not sure," I said.

Perhaps he read the surprise on my face and hastened to press his attack. "Surely you don't want to stay home on your first Friday evening in New York! We usually hit the clubs, the cool ones. You know, with Marco's Valentino pass we can get into places that..." Marco wasn't an intern like us; he had passed that stage a couple of years back and was on his way up the ladder toward a promising career. His position gave him some advantages.

"So who's coming? Marco, you and..."

"Relax, Marco will be there." Fabrizio's tone was teasing. His face had a smug, sassy look that irritated me. I decided not to play his game but he carried on, "Simone will be there too. He lives in the same place as Marco and I. He's a good guy."

"And who else?"

"Maybe your roommate. Is she cute?"

"Asena? She's nice, I get along fine with her, but on the weekend she sees her boyfriend."

"Then it'll be just us four. A 'Made in Italy' evening! You up for that?" With an automatic gesture Fabrizio tidied the papers on my desk.

"Sure I am," I replied as I moved a few files out of his reach. "Hands off," I added with a laugh. In response he tore a page from a notepad to write something on it.

"This is Pepita's address, the woman we stay with. Meet up with us there, we're close to Manhattan. From Queens, where you are, you have to take the red subway line. Make sure you don't get off at the wrong stop. Come on, let me get back to work now." Fabrizio thrust the crumpled sheet into my hand and headed off along the corridor. In that same moment I heard Marco's laughter rising over Rosario's voice. Perhaps the door of their office was open.

My thoughts returned to Fabrizio's mocking tone and I discovered that I wanted to run into Marco, or even just see him pass in front of the room I was working in. It occurred to me that I could try lying in wait for him in the kitchen, waiting for him to come in for a coffee.

In next to no time my head was full of Marco and I couldn't concentrate on anything else. It just happened, without any intention. Fabrizio had realized that before I did.

I sat there at the desk, like a dummy. A silly little girl. I don't know why but I thought of Forrest Gump, a character who I always found endearing. Perhaps I was Forrest, unwrapping one of my famous chocolates. Something was happening, something new and beautiful. I couldn't find the right words to define what I felt when I thought about Marco. It wasn't some kind of summer fever, the sort of thing that goes away quickly without leaving any trace. I was sure of that.

Marco, what had happened? There had been some everyday encounters over coffee and a couple of lunch breaks, running to catch the elevator together, laughing, and the two times he had stopped to ask me how things were going and to give me a few tips. Then he had told me I could count on him for anything I needed.

Marco. It had happened in a wholly unexpected way, nothing like the crushes I had had in the past. I who wanted everything under control, I who left nothing to chance and to reassure myself spent my life organizing every step of whatever there was to do, I had been taken by surprise. By what? I was afraid to admit it to myself: love had crept in, without any warning.

I had so many things to do, to experience. I wondered whether, rather than a beautiful thing, this affair might be an obstacle. I would be able to handle the matter. But what I felt left me open-mouthed, with a big smile on my face.

Could I hope I had found love? And what about him?

Together? The word together, Marco and I, Marco with me. In my thoughts.

And Fabrizio? He had made fun of me, although gently, for something I had not yet recognized. Perhaps someone else might have realized this?

I was overdoing it. Maybe it was all in my imagination, and I decided to take my mind off it by concentrating on work. Maybe it was less serious than it seemed.

I remembered that the evening before I left Italy I had been in the garden watering Mom's flowers, there had been an early heat wave. I was waving the hose around slowly, making flourishes on the flower bed and in the air. In my head I was already on the plane. My brother snatched the hose from me and gave me a good soaking. He was laughing, and I wanted to hit him. He had ruined my hairdo. I wished he were with me now, to dump some cold water over me. I needed to clear my head. I had to explore, to know, to build my future. I had never thought of love as an obstacle, something that takes away your clarity of mind. It was certainly only a passing thing. I should have eaten more at breakfast.

I raised my arm to sniff my elbow, something I always did when I wanted to play for time. With my face half covered I stared at the numbers running across the monitor and I tried to clarify the situation to myself. Was this just a crush? The same thoughts kept running around my head, and though the form changed little, the substance was identical. I liked Marco, I liked him a lot. I was falling in love, or maybe the fat was already in the fire. I felt sick.

Trembling with love for Marco.

I continued repeating this to myself all day long and even in bed in the evening. I couldn't sleep, I got up to get a drink and found that Asena was up, too.

"How come you're not in bed?"

"Homesick," Asena replied, as she sat at the table with a bowl of yogurt and cereal, a thick mush.

"You've been here for a long time now. You're a New Yorker. I envy you." I switched on the radio at low volume, The Soul Asylum were singing *Runaway Train*.

"Two years. No, a bit more. But that's not it. Tomorrow is an important day for me. David is introducing me to his family."

"So he means business!"

"Yes. He asked me to marry him and I'd like it if my parents were here." She swallowed a spoonful of the thick stuff and sighed deeply.

"I, I don't know...I think something has happened to me."

I hesitated to confide in her. I didn't know Asena well, and I would have liked to have Bea at my side. My friend would have brought me back down to earth. Eventually I made up my mind: "I think I'm in love. A guy at the office. His name is Marco." As soon as the words came out, my love grew stronger. It became real, concrete. Instinctively I reached out my hand, in front of me. I could almost see Marco, touch him.

Asena smiled, "Yes" she said. "So I see."

I went back to bed, but only managed to sleep for a few hours. I was too excited by the discovery that I was in love and the fact that Marco had not paid any particular attention to me was a mere detail. The distance between us didn't scare me.

That evening we would be going out together. It was a good start even though we wouldn't be alone. I didn't see him at all during the day. He, Fabrizio and Rosario Montrone were busy with a series of meetings. I would have liked to ask for other explanations on how to get to Pepita's place, but it didn't matter. I had the note with the address that Fabrizio had given me the day before. I would manage.

I didn't have the right dress. I needed something spectacular. An outfit that Marco would never forget. I talked to Zoe. She was French, and she had already been working for Valentino for several years and had an important job in marketing. Older than I, around thirty or maybe more, she was a prickly character who was treated with caution by most of my other colleagues. Yet she had taken a liking to me right from the first time we had met by the coffee machine. She said I reminded her of her younger sister, who had stayed in Franc to be a wife and mother. Zoe was always very eleg ten wore Valentino.

"Don't worry," she said in a mysterious tone. "I'll solve your problem, just don't make a habit of it."

"What do you mean?" Around us the air was thick with ringing telephones, the humming of printers, and the subdued chatter of colleagues.

"You'll see. Skip lunch today and come with me. I'm busy right now." Zoe turned away, leaving me to stew in my curiosity until one o'clock, when she suddenly appeared behind me. "Follow me, we have to go downstairs."

"Where are we going?"

"Listen, Anna. I don't do this kind of favor very often. Only for people who I like for some reason." She was walking fast along a secondary corridor, one of those into which I had never ventured. "Now you're in for a nice surprise. But make sure you don't disappoint me!" In the meantime, we had arrived at the service elevators.

"In what way?" I replied, going into the empty cabin.

"I will help you, but you must make your handsome Marco fall for you. It won't be easy, I believe. He's been here for two years and I've never seen him hit on any girl. He's a man who sticks to the rules and not flirting with the interns is one of them. The company doesn't look kindly on these things; in fact relationships between colleagues are *outlawed*. My feeling is that your man minds his business very far from the office." As she talked she constantly ran her fingers over the baroque pearl necklace that stood out over her electric blue outfit. "That means you must be careful. Do you understand me?"

The doors of the elevator opened onto a big room full of rows and rows of racks laden with dresses. With purposeful strides Zoe made her way through the labyrinth of fabrics, making them rustle with a sound that reminded me of the ripe grain in the field behind my house in Italy. She was walking fast, and as I followed her I caressed silks, linens, costly wools, lace, and inlays...I made sashes and belts sway, moved coat tails, and lifted feather-light tulles. They were in all colors. Valentino had invented shades that could not be translated into words; the scent of the fabrics was intense, hard to define, perhaps it resembled the smell of paper mixed with starch, and there was a subtle hint of leather too: the accessories. I was in such a whirl that when Zoe stopped, I crashed into her back.

"Excuse me!" She gave me a sidelong glance. I sniffed, like a little girl. I wanted to ingratiate myself, be her little sister.

"This is Alvin. This is Anna, an Italian friend."

"I adore Italian women!" Alvin smothered me in a vigorous hug that amazed me. He was rather small, and his head was on a level with my stomach. He had an exotic, very handsome face. I thought he was a wizard. I stood there in front of him, bemused.

"When do you need it for, baby?" he asked.

"For this evening." Zoe replied in my place. "Listen, Alvin, can you hand it in again on Monday? Come on, don't make her come here specially tomorrow morning, on a Saturday."

"It depends on what she takes." Alvin took a few paces back, almost swamped by the rack full of suits all in shades of sand that stood behind him. "Spread out your arms," he ordered. He was appraising me very carefully. "What does she have to do?" It was clear that he was speaking to Zoe again. Perhaps he had concluded that I didn't know how to speak.

"Goodness knows! A night on the town, I think. We want something elegant, but without going over the top. Original, though. It must be something memorable." Zoe winked at me. "We must make an impression. Do I make myself clear?" I didn't have time to respond.

"Let's see." Alvin was moving catlike through the racks of clothes. He chose three outfits. "These should fit you. Try them on and then we'll see about the accessories."

"Where can I try them on?" I asked, looking around for a changing room.

Zoe and Alvin burst out laughing. "Here. You'll have to do it in front of us. Like the models do." My friend stood there with folded arms. She had no intention of sparing me any embarrassment.

"Oh, these Italian women! They're always so bashful." Alvin gave me a mischievous look.

I was embarrassed, but I began to strip. Those two bore a sinister resemblance to the Cat and the Fox in *Pinocchio*.

# 6
## PEPITA'S HOUSE

A few hours later I emerged from the subway at 110th Street. I realized right away that something wasn't right. I took another look at the note with Fabrizio's scribbled directions on it; only then did I realize that I'd taken the green line instead of the red. I had arrived at 110th Street, but on the Lexington Avenue side, toward the east, instead of the Broadway side, to the west. There was nothing else to do but to skirt the north side of Central Park in order to get back on the right track. I wasn't that far from Pepita's house, I had just made the route a bit longer. If I walked at a good pace I would arrive at my destination in a quarter hour, twenty minutes at most.

It was almost nine in the evening on a hot June day and it was still a little light out. I felt as luminous as a star. Thanks to Zoe, Alvin had given me 'on loan' a Valentino outfit that was the most beautiful thing I had ever worn. It was made of, antique-rose silk. The cut was reminiscent of the clothes I had seen worn by Greek vestals in my schoolbooks. It was knee length, and had strange sleeves that left the shoulders bare and then covered the arms. Below the elbows they were decorated with little iridescent beads the same basic color as the dress. The matching shoes, with four-inch heels, were not suited to fast walking, at night, in a neighborhood that bordered on a disreputable one. I was near the point where Central Park ended. On that side it was all dark. On the other side was the start of Morningside Heights, the part before Columbia University; in the background a row of dilapidated buildings cast a long, compact shadow, useful for concealing the movements of groups of men wearing hoodies. Some were moving around furtively, or at least that's how it seemed to me then. No doubt more than one of them was a dealer. Luckily several people were out jogging and, near the subway, lots of kids were running around on skateboards.

It took me half an hour to reach my destination. I was warm after the long walk and I didn't slow down even on the final stretch, although I couldn't help noticing the show put on by the people who spent their evenings on the street. I saw they were almost all Latin Americans, as well as a few blacks. Some were sitting on the stoops, others on chairs set outside to enjoy the cool. Some had made a kind of concert and were playing and singing in groups, heedless of anyone who may have been listening and also of anyone inside the houses who may have wanted to rest. In the air there was a pungent odor of spices, garbage and smoke, a cloying mix that soon become nauseating. I rubbed my nose with my wrist and breathed in the comforting aroma of *Acqua di Giò*, my favorite perfume.

Ragged or half-naked children were playing, chasing one another and getting soaked under the fire hydrant that cooled the air, while I took care not to wet my dress. I flew up the steps to Pepita's house, annoyed at being late.

I pressed the buzzer and waited while from inside came the sound of running footsteps. I was amazed to realize I was nervous.

"You're gorgeous! Come on in, Anna, that's some dress..."

Fabrizio bombarded me with compliments as he led me along a rather bleak, dark corridor. At the end a shaft of light led to a half-open door.

"Come on in. This is Marco's cave and this is Simone, the third member of the Pepitas, to cut a long story short."

The first person I saw was Marco, who was bustling about at the table on which stood some bottles, mismatched glasses and a big bowl full of ice. He looked up and dispensed his usual warm smile, but didn't move. I felt he was distant, far away. I was disappointed and vexed at the same time.

Simone, instead, greeted me in an affected sort of way. "So, you're the famous Anna fresh in from Italy." He kissed me on the cheeks.

"I wouldn't say famous," I replied as I tried to reduce the distance between Marco and me.

"Oh, but you are famous," Simone shot back, drawing up a chair for me. "Fabrizio has done nothing but talk about you. He really did my head in."

"Where are you from? Are you from the Marche, too?" I asked. I wasn't interested in the turn the conversation was taking. I was angry because Marco had only given me one distracted glance while I had taken a lot of trouble to get ready for the evening and had come to his place full of expectations. I wasn't sure of what to do, or how to take this.

Simone grabbed another chair and put it in front of me, face to face. He straddled the chair and leaned against the back. He gazed at me and started talking again: "Naples, I'm from Naples. How could you not get that? Can you see any other good-looking guys like me in here?" I gave a loud laugh that drowned out his two friends' lighthearted protests. Only then did I look at him more closely. He was handsome, very handsome: tall with curly hair and dark eyes, amber-colored skin and an athletic body. But I was irritated by his hitting on me. Marco served the first round of margaritas, almost without looking at me, polite and indifferent. I was hurt by his detached manner, so different than the tingle I had felt when, on taking the glass, his hand met mine. Yes, this crush was something new and I would have done anything to find out where it might take me.

Who did he think he was dealing with, this Marco? I had the impression he was deliberately avoiding me. I was almost certain that if I touched him, even innocently, he would have withdrawn. Maybe he was one of those people who shunned physical contact; I knew some people were like that even though I had never met any. Maybe he was avoiding my gaze, but I wasn't sure of that. Perhaps Fabrizio had made some crack about me and the idea of an office affair had irritated him. Perhaps he liked me and didn't want to encourage me all the same. In any event, he was keeping me at a distance.

The guys launched into a rather dumb exchange of banter. I didn't feel entirely at ease and I was already wondering if I had been wise to accept the invitation when someone knocked at the door.

"Punctual as the angel of death." Fabrizio emphasized his words with a hand gesture and an eye roll.

"What a ballbreaker that woman is!" Simone slung his leg over the chair and went to open the door.

"Come on!" Marco said. "You know she's fond of us."

In the doorway a small, fat woman appeared. She was wearing a printed cotton slip dress decorated with improbable brick-red and yellow lozenges. Her features were unequivocally South American and I thought she might be Chilean. Instinctively, I got up and spoke to her in Spanish.

"Anna," I introduced myself. "Cómo está usted señora?"

"Muy bien mi hija...Pero que linda estas," she replied.

Fabrizio shot me an amazed look. "Well, we've no problems with Spanish then!"

"Anna is full of surprises," Marco said. "Pepita is our landlady. We all live here. Simone and Fabrizio each have a room off the corridor. But as I am the oldest tenant, Pepita has given me a whole apartment."

"No se burle," the woman replied. "No va a ser un palacio, es pequeño, pero es conveniente."

"How about going back to English, Pepita?" Simone was making fun of her, but his tone wasn't friendly. In his voice there was an ill-concealed arrogance that annoyed me.

"Excuse me! *Perdon*." Pepita smiled good-naturedly. She had a protective way about her. For a moment she reminded me of my mother.

"Come on, it's getting late." Marco laid his hands on my shoulder to propel me toward the door. I reached out to pick up the clutch I had left on the bureau; it wasn't on loan from Valentino, it was mine, bought at the flea market in Dolo: small and gilded, it looked like a little jewel box.

"Yes, Pepita, we're going out now. Maybe we'll go dancing." Fabrizio led her in a few dance steps and, laughing, she followed him.

"The night is young and we're going to enjoy it. Isn't that right, Anna?" Simone took my arm and led me out into the corridor. I turned around to look at Marco, who had hung back. He was paying no attention to me, and was hastily chugging down the umpteenth margarita. A moment later he came out into the corridor and fumbled with the keys to lock the door.

We took a ramshackle cab and Marco sat beside the driver, a wrinkly black man with leathery skin whose folds were tinged with the same blue as the night, and began to negotiate the price of the ride. I was sitting in the back, between Fabrizio and Simone, who were making too much noise.

"In Anna's honor we're going to take a tour," Marco cried triumphantly. The margaritas had gotten everyone a little drunk, except me because I only had one drink.

"Hang on tight, now! We're headed for Manhattan straight as an arrow, from north to south as far as Fourteenth." Marco resumed, his voice a tad out of sync, his high and low tones too emphatic. "My dear Anna, we're taking you to Midtown West, west of Times Square in the middle of Manhattan Island, the heart of New York. You'll hear its beat. Boom, boom, boom..."

"*I want to be a part of it, New York, New York...*" Fabrizio began to sing.

"Learn, Anna," Marco went on, his voice too high. "The West Side Highway is the road that runs west of Manhattan. By taking it, you get from the south side toward Downtown, where the action is, the *action*, get me? It's the fastest way to get to our favorite places. New York is ours, we rule it now, right guys?"

"Hot damn, you're right!" Fabrizio was beating his fists against his knees. Simone carried on singing, but he had turned down the volume. He shot me a sidelong look, a kind of sly smile.

"You know what my kingdom is, Anna?" Now Marco had turned toward us, his arms dangling over the seat and the seat belt looped over his back. The alcohol had loosened him up.

"The Meatpacking District, that's my kingdom!" he bawled. "With my pass I can get in anywhere."

"*These vagabond shoes are longing to stray...*" Now Fabrizio and Simone's chorus was in full song again. Marco winked at me and he and I started to sing too, "*Right through the very heart of it, New York, New Yooork...*" By this time the atmosphere of the evening had gotten to all of us.

I was euphoric. The Manhattan skyline was unfolding before me, the lights electrified me. I had the same feeling I used to get when, on a Sunday, I went to the carnival and my little girl's hand would try to get free of my father's grip so I could run to the rides.

Here the halo of the lights that blurred the outline of the skyscrapers, the buildings, the signs, the taxis and the trains, they all had the same consistency as the fog on certain November evenings, in the field behind my house. A variety of odors cut through air thick with dust: dirt, sand, ashes, face powder, sweat, skin, breath, fragments of life.

On this ride I could go round as often as I wished. I could hardly believe it.

The four of us began to go out frequently, almost a regular date. I would wait anxiously for the evening, while in the office I maneuvered to attract Marco's attention, with no success. He treated me nicely, with friendly familiarity. He even spoke to me with a certain protective air.

"It's not like I'm his sister," I confided to Fabrizio, who had understood before I did how hard I had fallen for his friend.

"Come on, don't take it badly." It was one o'clock and we were lounging on the usual bench in Bryant Park, taking in some sun as we ate our sandwiches. "Now I'm going to tell you a quasi-secret."

"A quasi-secret? What's that?"

"A secret you can share only with special people. The secret is Marco's and I'm sharing it with you. It's like a part of the thread that unites us or a scout's pact of blood brotherhood."

"What are you talking about?" I was laughing.

"I'm raving," Fabrizio replied. "Besides, it's only Wednesday. Have pity on me. I'm not Marco, after all. He lives to work, I work to live."

"Yes" I replied rather dreamily. "He's so serious."

"But when he came here he dumped his girl in Italy."

"..."

"Don't give me that worried look. He didn't leave her alone and pregnant. They broke up. He told me that the affair had gotten to be too much. They had been playing at lovebirds since high school. Her family was well off, I mean wealthy. Marco's wasn't. She was too demanding. The relationship was smothering him. He broke it off and two years ago, when they offered the first internship, he came here to try his luck. Cool, eh?"

"I don't know...Sure, if something isn't working. But what sort of a secret is that?"

"He doesn't want people to know. I know because back home we hung out together for years. Everyone knows everything about everyone else."

"I don't get it. Why doesn't he want..." I turned and leaned over the back of the bench and began to crumble the bread into the grass. I wasn't hungry anymore.

"He doesn't want a serious relationship anymore. You know, it hit him hard even though he was the one who broke it off." Fabrizio took a sip of water from the bottle in his backpack.

"So there's no way? For me, I mean."

He didn't reply right away. He seemed to be concentrating on the procession of passersby, an untranslatable sequence of ethnic groups, colors, sounds and even odors. Whatever he might say, I wouldn't have accepted the theory that perhaps I had no chance with Marco; in fact, what I had learned might be to my advantage. There was room for me, I was sure.

I waited in silence for Fabrizio to resume, "Since he's been here, Marco has done nothing but work, night and day. That's partly why he's already made a good career for himself. Not everyone can make it to a position like his in two years. But since I got here things have changed." He smiled at me, unsure if he should continue. In the end he said, with a self-important, macho air, "If he's enjoying life more now, then that's due to me. I made him rediscover a taste for fun. He goes out with models. He really loves Brazilian girls." I felt he was laughing about something he would never have told me. Men's secrets. For a moment I felt lost.

"But...In the long term you might make it. Eh, Anna, you have to play your cards well. Basically, Marco is the family sort. Come up with something, give him a taste of Italy again. And then...Are you aware that Simone has fallen for you?"

"Thanks, but I'm not interested in that item." I blushed, despite myself.

"He's an excellent catch, you know. His father is a lawyer, a tradition handed down from father to son. The guy is good looking and rich. Marco and I are penniless. All we have is our salaries. And I'm just a poor intern." He pretended to weep.

"Listen, Fabri..." At that moment my cell rang. It was Simone inviting me to the cinema that very evening.

# 7
# SIMONE

"It's impossible to get bored in New York." Simone was gazing at the waters of the East River as he talked. He lit his cigarette and drew heavily, filling his lungs with smoke. "This is
the most dynamic city in the world."

"The most dynamic? What's that? Have you seen them
all?"

"All what?"

"The other cities in the world."

"Silly girl!" He gave me a pat on the cheek and I had time
to smell the odor of tobacco on his fingers. I didn't like that.
Marco didn't smoke. Well, maybe the occasional joint. Like
everyone.

In the end I had accepted Simone's invitation with the intention of sending Marco a clear message. I had never desired
a guy so much in my whole life. I was possessed by a power
that, on the one hand drove me to act in ways I thought were
no part of me, while exasperating me on the other. For example, it wasn't like me to use a cheap trick like accepting the
courtship of another man who I had no feelings for just to
make Marco jealous while he carried on ignoring me.

I no longer thought about home, and I unceremoniously
broke off telephone conversations with my mother. She had

started to ask questions, suspecting that I had met someone special. I could tell from her overwrought tone.

Yes, yes, yes. My head was full of Marco, but I didn't want to let her know that. At least not yet. Besides, there was nothing to say, the affair hadn't got off the ground yet and goodness knows if it ever...

At work I tried to concentrate; this was no time to risk looking bad. Anyway, I was in New York because I had bet on myself and I was going to honor that commitment at all costs. I was my own number one fan.

Even at the cost of giving up Marco? I thought of my home, my room with the window looking over the field of grain, a wave tinged with blond in the summer, a basinful of fog in winter. I was seized by feelings of affection for the Anna I had been until a few weeks before and for the young girl who had started to dream of traveling the world when she was laid up in a hospital bed. My parents' mission was accomplished; I knew that even though they still hadn't realized I had flown the nest. I was deciding for myself, because I was the mistress of my own future.

I imagined Marco visiting my house. I would have to take things slowly with my folks. For them Marco would be a stranger, at least at first.

"Daydreaming?" Simone had finished his cigarette and had come up so close that I was enveloped by his tobacco smell. Instinctively, I drew back and he grabbed my waist. His hands went almost all the way around it. He had taken me by surprise and I had no time to react: he sat me on the parapet of the bridge. He was tall.

"Let me down."

"Scared?" he smiled, showing his teeth. My body cast a cone of shadow within the light of the street lamp above us.

His features under the contrasting light made me even more uneasy, but I managed not to show it.

"I have no head for heights," I said seriously. "Let me down."

I felt nausea welling up inside. He looked at me, puzzled. His grip was firm, but at the same time I thought that in a split second he could have pushed me over the edge. A crazy thought, which arose only because I didn't like him. I glanced at the black water flowing below. I closed my eyes and drowned in fear.

Eventually Simone brought me pirouetting down, light as a ballerina. "Right, I had forgotten you told us the other evening that you don't like flying. Sorry."

"You haven't said much about yourself. How did you end up here?" I didn't like his overly familiar manner. From now on I would keep him at a distance and I would no longer go out with him alone. By now being close to him got on my nerves and I couldn't wait for the evening to end. I wasn't going to tell him anything more about myself. I closed myself up in a transparent, impenetrable bubble, but I wasn't sure how to handle the situation.

"My father is an important lawyer in Naples. I'm rich, but the family keeps me on a short allowance," he said smugly, laughing. An arrogant guy. In the meantime, we walked on. Around us lots of people were out for a stroll. It was a rather warm evening. "Would you like me to introduce you to a few friends? They live near here." He noticed my hesitation. "They're Italian, you'll like them." Maybe he made a distinction between the various categories of friends? Italians with Italians and so on?

"Okay, as long as it's near here..."

"Only one block away." He took my arm and we set off.

"You know, I still haven't understood which company you work for?"

"Ha, ha! For the Lazy-Ass company." He patted my arm gently with his hand, as if to reassure me. Perhaps he had noticed that I had kept my distance after the prank on the bridge. I reacted with detachment to whatever he said or did.

"I get by," he resumed. "I did three months in a law office, then I went back to Italy and now I'm here again. I save money by living at Pepita's, and as for food, I just freeload. You know, I've lots of friends. My father thinks I'm still in the same law office." He took an antique silver pillbox from his pocket.

"Oh, that's pretty! May I see it?" I asked. "I love these old things." He stopped and handed it to me without speaking. The lid was engraved with initials I struggled to make out: R.T. "Whose is it?"

"It was my grandmother's, Renata. Inside there's a miniature portrait of grandfather Nando." We had stopped in front of a home appliance store. In the window there was a huge television showing the soccer teams that were to take part in the World Cup a few days later. We both stood there looking at the images of the Italian national team; Simone began to reel off the names of the squad. I wasn't interested, in fact, I was bored.

"What a romantic, your grandmother!" I flipped open the lid and fell silent. The box held a quantity of white powder, and inside the lid, the image of his grandfather was spattered with it.

Simone clasped my hand in his, closing the pillbox again. "I have a sister in Italy. My twin, to be exact. She loves me and every so often she sends me some money. In secret. Pocket money for my vices." He laughed, then added in a low voice, "Want some? You up for that?"

My head spun and I felt the first stab of a headache. I suddenly felt guilty about a mistake that in any case, I wouldn't have made. I still had to reckon with this feeling of sin that, at the most unexpected and inopportune times, would well up in my throat and then in my head. Not the result of any reasoning, it was a gut feeling. It was the legacy of my upbringing, catechism, customs, and of certain ways of thinking steeped in prejudices that didn't belong to me, but were still concealed deep down in the baggage I dragged along with me, despite myself.

"Well?" Simone was staring at me, looking shady. He would read nothing in my eyes.

"You've got it wrong" I replied curtly. "I'm tired. I'm getting a cab and I'm going home." I moved to the edge of the sidewalk and raised my arm.

"Come on, Anna! Let's at least finish enjoying the evening."

He was right beside me, and he took my hand. His disappointed tone was that of a little boy who has realized he isn't going to get the toy he wanted so much. In the meantime, a yellow cab had pulled up.

"It's okay." I shut the door with a smile and left him alone. A good thing it had all happened fast. I wasn't going to waste any more time with Simone, not even to make Marco jealous.

# 8
# THE VENETIAN GIRL

*New York, May 27, 2006*

That Saturday, the appearance of the new intern in the office had been an agreeable surprise. Anna Venier had brought in a breath of fresh air at a time when I really needed one.

Pretty, sure of herself, eager to feel at home, here as in Italy, Anna wasn't a hard type to understand. She was very straightforward and I have always liked people who aren't afraid to reveal their true selves. I felt immediately at ease with her.

"Okay, Anna. You have won a complete tour of the offices, so I'm going to introduce you to the people who are here today, all workaholics to the bitter end."

"Fantastic! I'm so glad to be here. How long have you been working for Valentino? How did you end up here?" I was comforted by the girl's cordial sincerity. "Excuse me, I know. You must think I'm nuts, but what do you expect...Did arriving in the Big Apple have the same effect on you?"

I noticed that as she talked she was moving to the rhythm of *Thievery Corporation*, the discreet sound track that pervaded the offices, the same one used for the last high fashion runway. I was so used to that background music that I didn't notice it anymore. I smiled at Anna's rapt expression at the sight of the big rooms full of cluttered desks, where many workstations were occupied even though it was Saturday morning. She behaved like all the Italians who won an internship with Valentino New York—they flew high and had a hard time landing. It had happened to me, too, in my time. I saw that she took to flight with particular grace.

"The idea of living in New York, even for a short time, makes everyone a bit crazy. You're lucky to arrive now, when the weather's nice. The main downside here is the climate, especially in winter, when it's freezing. Rent is a problem, too, and sometimes even more than a problem. How are you set up? Ah, here, this will be your place, as of Monday." She slipped onto the chair as if it were a throne, forgetting her surroundings.

"Hey, guys! Steve, Zoe, Alvin..." I tried to get the attention of the people sitting nearest. "This is Anna Venier, from Venice. She'll be here with us for three months. Longer if she's lucky." Heads looked up and a chorus of dissonant greetings rose up. Anna turned around and accompanied her smile with a wave. Zoe came over to introduce herself and started to chat, but I stopped her. "Okay, you'll get to know each other better Monday. Right now Anna is in the grip of the well-known *Valentino intern syndrome.* Let her savor this moment." It was an old line, but it got a few laughs all the same. No one made a rejoinder, besides, it was Saturday and they were all in a hurry for the weekend to begin.

Anna was sitting, gently touching the laminated surface of the desk and the keyboard of the computer, which was off. She moved the mouse here and there, another flight test. "Fantastic, it's all fantastic!" she said dreamily.

A nice little girl. I filed her away. "If you're through making love to the job, let's go for coffee."

"Sure! I'm making you waste time." She blushed at my teasing. "I'm so happy...to be in New York and to have met Italian friends. Are there others who work here?"

"More than you can imagine. Lots of Italians and lots of other people from all over the world."

"But are any of them...New Yorkers?"

"I know a couple and I've been here for two years." It was satisfying to make fun of her.

"What are they like?"

"New Yorkers? On the surface they are positive, optimistic. They're always in a rush, like everyone else. But if you scratch that surface, I'd say they're dissatisfied. Living in this city means taking a run up and then never stopping. In the same way, all of us..." Anna was staring at me. I stopped. "Right, we're here. This is our kitchen."

"It's small!"

"What did you expect? A bar?"

"Oh, there's a Lavazza coffee machine!" She was actually moved. A few hours out of Italy and her enthusiasm was already veined with an aftertaste of homesickness. "It has gilded edges!"

"Where are you from, exactly? Venice?"

"No, from a small town a half hour from there. It's almost country, with rows of factories, fields, a little church and a whole lot of fog in winter." She gave an embarrassed laugh.

"Well, it's well known that the Veneto is like that: factories and wine," I replied. "In a certain sense, we who come here to work are all from the Veneto, or Milan, if you like. Even people like me who come from the coast."

Anna pushed away the paper coffee cup and smiled. A little coffee smudge was printed on her upper lip. The Venetian girl was a real character, no denying it.

I was to get to know Anna better, but at first I didn't want anything to do with her. A possibility to be nipped in the bud, a potential danger. But Fabrizio never missed a chance to kid me about her. I suspected he liked her, too.

"By the way, Marco, you know that the cutie went out with Simone yesterday evening? Doesn't that bother you?"

"No, it doesn't bother me. Why should I be interested in her?" I was dumbfounded. I was in a crammed subway car with Fabrizio, only one stop before we got off for the office.

"Well, because she's crazy about you. Come on, if you haven't noticed that you're real dumb."

"I'm out," I replied, opening my eyes wide. "But what a Judas you are, Fabri. I really didn't see your game."

"And that would be?"

"I thought you were interested in our new recruit and that you were even a bit jealous. Instead, you're acting as her mentor. You've given yourself away. Fine friend you are." In the meantime, the train had begun to brake and I was making my way to the doors, still followed by Fabrizio.

"Mentor? I'm no mentor. Do you mean to tell me that you haven't noticed how she's all over you and does all she can to get your attention? And you, what do you do? She's smart, you know. Anna is a good kid, I'm telling you."

Now we were on the platform, amid the flood of commuters. I didn't say anything more. I had no desire to go into things any deeper. He could talk and say all he wanted to, but I was going to stay out of this business. Of course I knew that Anna liked me and I kept her at a distance for that very reason. I didn't want complications because I realized that something had clicked between us. Whatever it was, I wasn't up for it.

I had caught certain looks of hers...I was sure that those glimpses into her soul were reserved for me only, but I wasn't about to take advantage of them.

I liked my job, the days tailored to work, the circular thoughts about my commitment to the company and my career, the occasional night out when I could have fun without restrictions, then off to bed for a dreamless sleep with no worries. No, I had no room for Anna, or for anyone like her. I was going to steer clear of love affairs, serious ones at least. My life was fine as it was. In the meantime, we had come up onto the street and began to walk against the flow of the compact mass of people advancing like a wall in the direction of Times Square. We were on 42nd Street, near the office, when I spotted two kids leaning against a lamppost and kissing, without any embarrassment. As if they were alone.

The sight of them irritated me.

I rejected the feeling of being holed up in a life too big for myself alone, where there was a lot of empty space. Sometimes my thoughts wandered on their own account, leading me in directions I wouldn't have liked to take. Every so often, I would go back in time, to home, when my mother was still alive. Not that I was homesick for Italy and my family, not the way it was now. My only regret concerned my mother, who had enjoyed so little. When she died I suffered more than my brother, or rather, I struggled more than he did to get over the bereavement. I was the younger child—I was only fifteen, and I had a special bond with her. This certainly had to do with my childhood illness, a tumor that had cost me a kidney. Just enough time to understand that I'd had the narrowest of escapes, a handful of years in which we were like two young lovers, and then she had to die in a traffic accident.

Fate, they say.

I had grown up alone—that was the truth. With my father and my brother I had made my smile my banner, as I do now. If you smile, people accept you more easily and maybe they even come looking for you.

A smile is an expression people like.

I didn't need anyone with whom to share my feelings, my secrets. Maybe one day, but not now. I had goals to attain. Better to concentrate on work and forget the rest. As soon as I got to the office I said goodbye to Fabrizio and dove headlong into the paperwork: budgets, accounts and forecasts, numbers. When I eventually allowed myself a coffee break, I found Fabri lying in wait for me in front of the Lavazza coffee machine.

"Have you seen her today?" He was a guy who didn't let things go. "Bumped into her? She's not here," he continued, undaunted.

"Listen, Rosario will be here in ten minutes and I still have to finish my report. I don't know anything else." I went off with the paper cup in my hand.

I've known Fabri since we were small. We grew up in the same bunch of kids and we had shared many first times together: the first furtive cigarette, the first trade in second-hand comics, communion and confirmation in the same neighborhood church, school, cutting classes, exams...We even had a crush on the same girl. Each of us managed to give her our first kiss, obviously at different times and occasions. Then we lost touch—I went to university in Ancona and he went to Urbino. He graduated after me.

"I wonder how it went with Simone? Aren't you curious?" He had followed me into the corridor.

"Nooo." I had no intention of playing his game. "Look, Rosario really is about to arrive. So scat," I said, making faces at him. "Go pretend to work." I invited him to clear out with a hand gesture and he responded with a silent Bronx cheer.

The same old Fabrizio.

New York and Valentino had taken us back a few years. He had arrived to try his luck with an internship and we were instantly back on the same wavelength, just like the old days. Getting together again was great, but my friend was too intrusive, or perhaps I was the one trying to defend the model of life I had built here. I tried to stay in my shell, but Fabri kept on provoking me.

In the previous two years I had forgotten that there were other things apart from my career and he had noticed that right away: "Marco, I don't recognize you. I've been here for a week and all I see you do is work. That's bad for you, you know." He was joking, but not that much.

"Really?" I had replied, not very convinced. One evening he managed to drag me out of the office at cocktail hour and forced me into a bar near our place. Fabri ordered two glasses of prosecco. They brought it with ice. Fabri didn't even comment on this, he was so busy handing me a lecture. "Now that I'm here you'll straighten up. I'm going to change your life." He shoved the prosecco away, watered down by now. "You show me the right places and I'll show you how to have fun again. Okay?"

I thought about it. "Work comes first," I said pompously, then I clinked my glass against his in a toast. Fabrizio had brought with him a breath of home and something had melted inside me. I had understood for some time that I belong to the category of people who have one foot in both camps, Italy and New York, which is not America. "To tell the truth, work is all I have. All I still have left," I concluded in an undertone. I was constantly swirling the wine around, and there was no ice left in the glass.

"I see," Fabrizio said, even though he couldn't have heard my final remark. "I'll see to it, let's begin right now. We'll have a proper drink and then find a decent place to eat. I've had it with Pepita's cooking. She's been mothering you for two years. She told me herself." He didn't give me time to reply and shoved the glasses aside before getting up and going to the bar to order. From that evening on we began to go out together two or three times a week and Simone often came along, too. We went to happening places to pick up girls. My Valentino card opened lots of doors. We hit the booze a bit too hard, Simone did other stuff too, but it's not as if we got very far. Every so often we'd hook up with some girl, sometimes even a few models. I had a weakness for South American girls with amber skin. Some of them were up for it, too, but there was the problem of where to go. Many girls turned up their noses at Pepita's address and, in the best of cases, even those who agreed didn't like having to sneak into the house like thieves, taking their shoes off so as to make no noise. If Pepita had woken up she wouldn't have taken it kindly. Living there meant respecting strict rules and the rooms weren't great, but on the other hand, they were real cheap. Finding an alternative was not easy. The girls often shared not only apartments, but also rooms, to save money.

Anna's arrival in the group was a pleasant diversion, but it hadn't changed our habits. She was smart, good company, and pretended to enjoy the customary little shot, but I saw straight off that she was the type who goes in for fruit juice and organic products. I kept telling myself that a girl like that wasn't one of my objectives. I didn't want anything to shake up my life, yet every now and then I found myself hoping to meet her in the corridor, in the elevator or in front of the coffee machine.

The more she came into my thoughts, the more detached I was with her. Basically, I liked the hint of disappointment, a subtle veil light as face powder, which fell over her face whenever she sought my attention and I deliberately ignored her. I read Anna like an open book, even though I didn't know her and felt an infinite tenderness for her. For that very reason, I wasn't going to lead her on.

In any case, I had come to New York to put an ocean between my past and my present and to have nothing more to do with Italian women. I had outgrown my home, and the future I could glimpse in Italy wasn't the one I dreamed of. But I didn't know where my real home would be one day; I couldn't imagine it. Maybe that has always been the fate of migrants; anyway I was sure I would have all the time I needed to find it.

I had decided to move on when my love story with Marcella, which had begun in high school, came to an end. Everyone who knew us was certain we would get married. She was pushing me to commit to making a comfortable future for us. She wanted to be the wife of a man with a position worth having. It seemed that marriage was her only goal in life. Marcella threw that in my face every time the talk turned to the possibility of a future together. She led the dance, and the more I hedged, the more she showed her authoritarian side. I began to feel stifled.

In my town, one of many on the Adriatic coast, if you come from a poor family, it's not easy to change things. If you're not someone's protégé, if you don't have the right connections, the best you can hope for is a slow uphill progress and often you don't even cross the finish line. Anyway, in Italy it's always been that way. Rosario, my boss, said the same thing. He left Sicily dirt poor and in New York he struck it rich thanks only to his own capacities.

Despite the distractions, I was done checking the report I was writing. I saved the document and sent it to the printer, then I got up to go to the Xerox in the opposite corner of the office. The clock said 10:50. I had finished early and could take a break while I waited for Rosario to arrive.

I turned toward the window. My New York was there for me, as always, just like that morning a couple of years before. It had been summer then, too, and two weeks after that my internship with Valentino was due to end. I would have had to go back to Italy. I laid my hands against the glass and the memory of what had happened floated to the surface.

"Marco, I'll expect you in Bailey's office in fifteen minutes." Rosario towered above my workstation of those days, close to the one Anna was occupying today.

"Me? Bailey's office?" I couldn't believe it and I was already excited; he had vanished along the corridor without further explanation. The clock said 10:45. I got up and went to the men's room, avoiding my colleagues' curious looks. I tidied myself up and stopped in front of the mirror to study my face. I was me, but extraneous to myself. So I decided to get into character; I had to make an effort to get over that feeling you have when you wake up in the morning and you don't really know where you are.

With an effort I focused on my image. I was sorry I didn't have a tie. I never wore one because I had always thought they were a pointless, annoying accessory, but for a summons to the office of Jim Bailey, the CEO of Valentino's American head office, a tie would have fit the bill. I thought of getting hold of one, but in the end I dropped the idea. 'I am what I am,' I thought. 'If they've decided they're interested in me, it means that I'm fine as I am.' Instead of going directly to the appointment, I went back to my desk and hung around there for a couple of minutes, for no reason. My colleagues nearby were observing me, some with a touch of envy in their eyes. They were all waiting for me to say something. I made a sort of grimace and spread my arms wide, as if disarmed before what I had to face. The response was a few good-natured insults and a few good luck wishes.

Eventually I decided to take the corridor that led to the elevator.

I pushed the button for the thirtieth floor.

I had never been in Bailey's office, I had only heard about it. When his assistant opened the door, I felt as if I were suspended in the air. Two entire walls were made of glass, and the space was enormous.

"Come on in." The CEO was in the command seat behind a glass desk. He gestured for me to take a seat in the chair facing him. Rosario was already seated beside me; he was laughing up his sleeve.

"Impressive, isn't it?" Bailey said. "Everyone who comes in here for the first time is stunned." He made a sweeping gesture with his hand as if he wanted to caress the space in which floated two conference tables and two areas with couches, a bar and a corner fitted out with some fitness machines: an exercise bike, a weight bench and a treadmill. Beyond the glass walls, the panorama, certain aspects of which were similar on both sides, was nonetheless different. Different even from that of Rosario's office and my own, a few floors below, which was spectacular, too.

Here we were in flight.

The day was rather hot and while on the one hand the sky was almost cobalt blue, on the other clouds like soft white dough notched the outlines of the skyscrapers. Lower down the air was yellow. There was nothing usual in what I was seeing. New York was a great whore—I had always known that. When you arrive, an Italian migrant of the latest generation, a young hopeful with no contacts and no means, she welcomes you with legs wide open in the filth of a hovel in which you would never have imagined you'd be obliged to live. If you're smart and lucky, you manage to find a place in the outer city, but you work in Manhattan and you play in SoHo. Only if you make the big step up and come out on top, among the clouds, does she reveal her true soul to you and then, maybe, you are granted the power that gives you the illusion of happiness.

"Excuse me. I don't know how to describe..."

"It would have been strange if you could." Bailey replied. "Sometimes it still happens to me, too." He dropped that remark as if it was an admission; maybe he was talking to himself. Then he stood up, placed his hands on the desk and, looking me right in the eye, he said, "Good, let's get down to our business."

Christ, what a day that had been. They offered me a steady job as Rosario's assistant and had me understand that they were going to keep a special eye on me. In the end, Bailey ended the conversation with a question: "Well, do you accept?"

And how could I have refused, sitting in that office with those two big cheeses and my spirit hanging suspended outside the windows? I was no longer Marco Falcioni, an intern from the Marche trying his luck in New York. Now I was Marco Falcioni, a man who, after many sacrifices, had made it. I was a part of the Valentino team. Perhaps I was fated to remain here. I was going to have other special moments like that, I felt it.

I was in New York and now it was my home. Would I ever pull up stakes and leave here? I didn't know. An airplane crossed the sky. I shivered because it seemed too close.

I was wrong, luckily; anyway, the time for reminiscing was up. The Xerox was through printing. I went back to the computer and the first thing I did was check the mail. There was a message from Anna addressed to Fabrizio and me.

> Ciao Marco, ciao Fabri!
> How long is it since you ate Italian last? I'll expect you tomorrow evening at my place. Bring the wine.
> Anna

The address followed.

Right, the girl had her fingers in the pie, so to say. She had told me she liked cooking when we first met, that Saturday morning when she had come to test the waters in the office. She had been moved at the sight of the Lavazza coffee machine and we had discussed how much coffee you need for a tiramisu.

Who knows, maybe she would give it to us as dessert tomorrow evening.

"We're going, right?" Fabrizio had popped up from nowhere. His tie was loosened and his hair untidy.

"Do you *never* work, really?" I felt like laughing, but resisted. "I don't know. Janina still has to confirm our date. You know, the model who's the spitting image of Laetitia Casta." Fabrizio said nothing, but his expression resembled the mask of tragedy. "Okay, just because I love you. We'll go to Anna's," I said.

"You're giving up Janina to eat Italian? Great, Marco! I would never have thought..."

"Indeed, don't think it. I would never have done it. Thing is, unfortunately, there's nothing going on with Janina. You know, I would, but she's not into me." As I was speaking I finished binding my report. I heard Rosario talking to someone. He was coming and must have been at the far end of the corridor.

"You shit, you're a real shit," Fabrizio said fondly, in a low voice. "Did you see the address? I hadn't realized...But where the hell is Anna staying?"

"In the wrong side of Queens. Come on, beat it now." Rosario appeared in Fabrizio's place, impeccable in an ash-gray suit. He bowed his head, "After you," he said, then he moved from the doorway to let a woman enter: Anne Hathaway.

I was left glued to my workstation. Rosario gave me a look that was complicit and amused at the same time. He made the introductions, but she didn't deign so much as look at me. We were all waiting to see her in *The Devil Wears Prada*. In the flesh she was magnificent.

"Excuse me," I said. "Rosario, here's the report."

I waved the folder in which I had closed it, then set it on the edge of the desk and he gave me an imperceptible nod as he took his leave. A buzz of suspicion came from the corridor. After all, our floor was reserved for the company's financial offices. Someone like Anne Hathaway had never been seen here before.

Upon leaving the room I closed the door. Outside there was a group of colleagues who were whispering, their curiosity aroused. Anna was there too, deep in conversation with Zoe and Fabrizio. That day she was wearing her hair up. Her neck looked like Audrey Hepburn's in *Breakfast at Tiffany's*.

84

# 9
## White Hydrangeas

I had been bustling about in the kitchen for almost three hours, not counting the time spent looking for the right ingredients for the dinner I had in mind. When I had arrived, Asena had shown me the tableware at our disposal; now, faced with my bewildered look, she burst into laughter in that strange way of hers, mumbling and breathing in through her mouth. She was beginning to irritate me, but I didn't show it.

"What do you expect? Silver underplates?" she asked.

"No. But here nothing is matched. Are there any serving dishes, at least? Any bowls?" I moved the dishes around on the table trying to make pairs of them.

"Have you invited your colleagues to dinner or are you expecting the president and his wife? Maybe I misunderstood..."[2]

"Come on, Asena. I need to look good. You know that. Marco will be coming. In Italy it's important for women to be good cooks. Men..."

"Oh my! Do you think I don't know how to cook? If you had listened to me I would have made my famous mezes and then..."

"I have to cook *Italian*," I almost spelled it out. "But don't you have to go out to choose your wedding list?"

"Yes, and I'm late too. How do I look? Is my hair okay? I'm off, and I don't know if I'll be back tonight." I made a face and she responded with a mischievous smile and a gentle punch on the shoulder, then she took her bag and left.

I recovered my calm and laid out the Flanders linen table-cloth with big white and gray stripes; I had bought it for the occasion from Anthropologie and it had cost me a bunch. I thought about how to arrange the mismatched china to ob-tain a harmonious effect or at least an acceptable one. Most of the dishes were vintage, with different shapes. The prettiest plates were patterned with little flowers with a geometric mo-tif and gilded edges. There was a pair of matching serving dishes and a few bowls in different colors. In the end I man-aged to put together an amusing, pleasing table, and certainly a rather peculiar one. I consoled myself by thinking that per-haps my guests might find it sophisticated.

In the middle of the table I placed a couple of candles and a vase of white hydrangeas that gave off a delicate scent. I had been very uncertain about the choice of flowers. The Chinese deli also had a florist's corner. I had struggled to decide on the right flower for my dinner. I sniffed, breathing in lustily as I tried to match forms and colors. In the end I fell for the white hydrangeas, they were extremely fresh and emanated a sense of intensity. They had always had that effect on me. My moth-er taught me that you never give hydrangeas to your beloved, because the bright colors of its blooms signify a desire to run away. But I had bought them for myself, to make the table pretty, and anyway, the white would prevent any disagreeable interpretations.

Marco and Fabrizio were due to arrive in ten minutes. I slipped on a very simple little dress the color of magnolias, touched up my makeup, let my hair down and put on the inevitable heart-shaped

Tiffany earrings, a kind of good luck charm. I was giving my lips a final touch of lipstick when the bell rang.

"You *do* know you're living in the midst of wolves?" Fabrizio had a scandalized air. "What's more it's miles from the office."

"How long does it take you to go there and back?" Marco asked, hammering the point home. "Do you realize that this is not a very safe neighborhood?"

"The apartment is nice, though," I said.

"True, but any apartment occupied by women is nice. Especially in comparison with the rooms in which men stay." Fabrizio was looking around, fingering Asena's photograph holder.

"Yes, our place can't compare. Anyway, you've seen where we live. Luckily Pepita is a good landlady and she helps us out." Marco put two bottles on the table. "The prosecco is in your honor. The Verdicchio dei Castelli is in ours. We'll put the prosecco in the fridge."

Fabrizio was already seated at the table and was feeling the tablecloth. "Did you bring this from Italy? My mom has them in this fabric, too. I don't remember what it's called..."

"Flanders linen. It's a Flanders linen tablecloth and I bought it here. We're in New York after all. It's a classic. Isn't it, Marco?" As I was talking I brought in the finger food. I had made salmon crostini, little rolls of asparagus with prosciutto, cubes of tomato frittata, bruschetta with cherry tomatoes and baby mozzarella. Tasty stuff, just to whet the appetite.

"Are we expecting anyone else?" Fabrizio looked famished and was helping himself to everything. Marco too, for that matter.

"No," I replied. "It's just the three of us."

"Thought so. I get the feeling you've made enough for an army. But that's fine by me. It's the first decent meal I've had since I arrived here."

In the meantime, I got up to fetch the other dishes from the kitchen. Marco followed me.

"Give me something to take to the table." Then he added in a low voice, "At home we have tablecloths like that. We never take them out. My mom died when I was fifteen. An accident." He turned around and went back to the table, to Fabrizio, who was stuffing himself. I was soon to discover that Marco had a healthy appetite, too. I was happy because he had told me something about himself. An important thing. He had confided in me and we had established a contact. Everything would go well; I felt that a spark had been ignited and now it was up to me to fan it.

Marco, Marco, Marco! I went back to the table holding a big red ceramic bowl.

"What's in there? Fabrizio was pouring wine for everyone. The bottle of water hadn't even been opened.

"A salad, to introduce..."

"Introduce what? A surprise?" Marco was collecting the plates of finger food, all empty.

"Even though it's summer, I've made lasagna for the first course. I thought..."

"May God bless you," Fabri cried.

"Yes, may God bless you. I suspected as much, by the aroma. I'll get it. You stay there." Marco was already on his feet.

"Stop! First the salad."

"What the hell, Anna?" Fabri was brandishing his fork like a trident, and on his face the expression of a child who was been told he was getting no ice cream.

"Wait." Marco took the bowl from my hand and sat down again. "Anna, take it easy. I'll serve you. What's in this salad?" He looked puzzled as he tossed the ingredients.

"Try it, it's really good. I put in iceberg lettuce with green apples, feta and *bagigi*. The oil is from Tuscany."

"*Bagigi?*"

"What the hell are *bagigi?*" Fabri stuck his fork directly into the bowl.

"What do you call them? Back home in the Veneto, *bagigi* is what we call peanuts." Laughing, I took a spoon and fished a peanut out of the bowl. "*This* is what I mean, you dummies." The wine had warmed up the atmosphere even though there was no real need. We all began to laugh about the peanuts.

"You made that up. *Bagigi!* Never heard the word," Marco said as he transferred a portion to his plate.

"It doesn't matter, forget it. The Venetian girl cooks fantastically well. Cut her some slack, let her invent all the words she wants." Fabrizio mumbled with his mouth full. "Surely you don't mean to say she invented peanuts."

I was laughing so much my eyes were watering, like my guests' for that matter. It was a pleasantly warm evening, and the wine and the food had brought about an atmosphere of home that we three, more than others, could appreciate. I was almost prepared to admit that *bagigi* was a phony word I had made up myself, even though that wasn't so. I wiped my eyes with a napkin, and the mascara left a mark on it.

"You're pretty just the same," Marco reached out a hand and ran his finger gently around the outline of my eyes. I felt like I was melting.

"*Bagigi* don't exist, do they?" he whispered

"They exist." I pretended to get mad. "Or at least they exist in my family's vocabulary," I stated with scarce conviction. I wasn't interested in that. Sitting at the table set with mismatched dishes, I was cheerful, in fact euphoric, because I was with two guys who were my friends. I felt that I had scored a major point thanks to the peanuts.

Especially with Marco. We were joking; the words didn't matter, it was the *way* we talked to one another, the gestures absorbed in graceful movements. He came toward me, I drew back smiling, but it was as if I had blown him a kiss.

Between one dish and the next there was a moment of silence.

"You've fattened us up." Fabrizio was red in the face, his voice hoarse, his expression tipsy.

"Think of it as a Sunday lunch Italian style." I immediately regretted that allusion. "Do you have any sisters, Marco?"

He brought out his wallet and took out a photo: "This is my family." On a pebbly beach, sitting on a pedal boat there was an elderly man, certainly Marco's father, and two youngsters. There was also a pretty girl in a bikini, with ash-blonde hair.

"What a lovely family. A brother and a sister..." He interrupted me right away: "It's not my sister, it's Sofia, my big brother Matteo's fiancée. This is me, the baby of the family," he concluded, taking back the photo.

"Neither of you look like your father," I said.

"Not one bit" Fabrizio broke in. "They're both the image of their mother. Don't you have a photo, Marco?"

Marco was already holding the photo of a young woman, a close up of a fine oval face, wavy shoulder length hair, regular features. A classic beauty who struck you for the melancholy power of her gaze.

"Your mother?" I said. "You both look really like her. A beautiful woman."

"She always said that we two were the masterpiece of her life." Marco put the photo back in his wallet very carefully, so as not to spoil it. There was such deep affection in the way he did it that I was moved.

I daydreamed for a moment, losing myself in a fantasy about the idea of such an intense and gentle tenderness devoted to me alone. It was worth the effort of cultivating what was coming into being, at all costs.

I have a confused memory of what happened afterward. We laughed a lot more, making fun of one another. There were a few cracks about our colleagues in the office. Fabri talked about his girlfriend in Italy. Marco knew her. I realized that those two had shared a lot of things and I envied them. I said something about my family, my home, but I said nothing about the accident that had changed my life. It would have been like showing Marco the scars I bore on my body. I wasn't ready for that; the right occasion would come along later on. It was a serious moment. I had just served the fruit salad of strawberries and watermelon, flavored with mint leaves.

"You all love one another in your family. You have a bond," Marco said with a hint of wistfulness that I didn't know how to interpret.

"Yes. I have a lovely family."

"I'm bursting." Fabrizio massaged his belly.

"But it's not over," I announced as I headed for the kitchen once more.

"Do not tempt me further, woman. We can't handle it." Fabri was rocking in his chair, his belt loosened. Marco pretended to be horrified by the prospect of having to eat anything more.

"One last thing. I made my special tiramisu with macaroons and mascarpone cream. And look out because I have thought up something new." I took from the fridge three jars of *Bonne Maman* jam, with the classic red and white checked lids. Fabrizio and Marco looked at each other and burst out laughing.

"Individual portions?" Fabrizio feigned desperation.

"I have a baking tin full in the fridge, if you want more."

"The recipe? You haven't invented anything strange, by any chance?" Marco was almost drooling.

"Well, it's my personal recipe, I told you. I have alternated the layers of macaroon steeped in American coffee with mascarpone cream." I handed round the jars. I had attached a little label to each one with our names. On Marco's label I had added a heart. I was still sowing my little pebbles.

"I want to dieee," Marco said.

"Me too," Fabrizio echoed him. "But only after eating at least another two portions."

# 10
## Forza Italia!

*New York, June 2006*

I saw Marco again the next day when I bumped into him in front of the elevator, together with other colleagues. I had to resist hugging him, and he limited himself to gratifying me with a smile, a compliment on my culinary skills and...headed down the corridor before disappearing into his office. In the hours that followed, he didn't seek me out nor did I have the chance to meet him at the coffee machine. I began to fear that he was avoiding me once more.

Maybe I had made a mistake. After the dinner at my place I had convinced myself that I had attracted his attention; I didn't think I had landed him, not yet, yet I hoped he would no longer think of me as the younger sister of the group. Buoyed up by my convictions, that morning I had left home with a swing in my step and now I was overwhelmed by disappointment.

I reviewed the memories of my previous loves. The list was short and maybe defining them as loves was going too far; they had been fancies more than anything else, crushes, two people with an intense interest in each other. And not even too deeply felt, to tell the truth, at least on my part. Yes, in Chile with Rodrigo, the student, there had been a blaze of passion, but the flames were fed above all by the result of chatting with my girlfriends, the many conversations we had about something with little in the way of substance. It was the idea, the dream of love, the way we invented it in our heads. The music that sang of it, the movies full of kisses, the books that talked of it and the secrets kept by couples older than us. We were merely adolescents in love with the allure of love.

With the Italian guys I had known things hadn't worked out so well. I didn't like them enough, that was the real reason why I eventually dumped Giacomo, a fellow student from Sicily who I had been sort of keen on for several months. It had been a painless farewell with few regrets. You move on, you think about it a bit and then you go to sleep and tomorrow is another day.

My mother always used to laugh at me when, faced with some problem, after having looked at it from all angles and having vainly sought a solution, I would decide to put any decision off until the next day. "I'm off to bed, Mom. Tomorrow is another day."

"Right, best sleep on it," she would reply. "Good night, Scarlett." She saw in me the spirit of the leading lady of Gone With The Wind, saying that it was a good thing to embrace her pragmatic, selfish philosophy because that way I would always land on my feet.

Nothing in my experience was comparable to my feelings for Marco. I tried to create silence within myself, but life in New York left little room for reflection. My days were frenetic; I was absorbed by my work, although it was a struggle to concentrate. A couple of times I went out with the group of interns, but the other evenings were a fixed date with Marco, Fabrizio and, sometimes, Simone.

My thoughts were getting more and more like my dreams and were concentrated on a sole subject, always the same one: Marco. He was the center of all my emotions, and all the other things outside or around him, work, colleagues, the glittering city, everything else was a mere accessory. I remained at a distance from reality and from those things in which others were the main players—even events that concerned the rest of the world, good or bad as they might be.

In the meantime the soccer World Cup had begun.

On June 12, a Monday, we organized an extra night out on the occasion of Italy's first game, against Ghana. We all went to Serafina, an Italian restaurant that had a giant TV screen for clients. The atmosphere was one of moderate excitement, partly because there were some among us who weren't big soccer fans and partly because an Italian victory was taken for granted. And in fact the game ended two–nil for Italy. There were quite a lot of us and I was sitting rather far from Marco and Fabrizio. For some of the time I watched the game and rooted for the team along with the others and for the rest I concentrated on Marco. 'Turn around, look at me.'

I tried to use telepathy, even though I knew nothing about it and even though I didn't even really believe in it. 'Marco, I'm here for you. Look at me. Can you hear me, Marco?' I was consumed by the effort of trying to link his thoughts to mine, across that big table cluttered with beers, mineral water, and dirty plates with the remains of pizza and spaghetti with meatballs. Not to mention the people and the unholy din they were making as they watched the game unfold on the screen.

I remember the two goals well because on both occasions the telepathic flow I had tried to activate was shattered by the shock wave of the exultant yelling of the Italians in the restaurant. One time Marco turned in my direction, toward the end of the first half. I smiled and he smiled back, then he turned around on his chair and spoke to the girl sitting at the table behind ours. They chatted for a while and even started giggling in a knowing and rather coarse way. I had the disagreeable impression that they might have been doing so at my expense. That was certainly the fruit of my imagination; I didn't want to accept Marco's lack of interest in me. I couldn't go on humiliating myself that way. I was never going to embarrass myself anymore, not even with *myself.*

My stomach was in a knot and my ears were ringing. I decided—no more Marco and no more evenings in company. But, when I got home, and it was already late, I didn't go to bed. I started bustling about in the kitchen.

"Anna, what are you doing?" Asena appeared wearing only a tank top and panties, her hair like straw. She was mad.

"Excuse me. I didn't mean to wake you. I made it as quietly as I could." I closed the oven and gave her a big smile, hoping to mollify her.

"Made what?" she yawned rudely.

"Orange cookies with fennel seeds. A recipe of my mother's. Want to see?" I stepped to one side to let her see the inside of the oven.

Asena stretched and held her arms up, almost brushing the top of the doorframe. She was a sweet girl and it didn't take much to pacify her.

"I want to sleep," she mumbled. "If you can't seduce him with food it means you're not the great cook you think you are." She turned back toward her room, her slippers shuffling.

A few hours later I left on Marco's desk a package wrapped up with a patterned ribbon whose predominant colors were white, red and green. The note said that I had made the cookies to celebrate the national team's victory. They were enjoyed by lots of people, not just Marco, as I had hoped. He thanked me, rather curtly. I swung between anger and justification of his conduct because he had to avoid gossip in the office, but even outside, it wasn't as if he treated me any differently.

There were other games, but the script was the same: I tried to get a seat near Marco and, when I thought I had managed that, someone always snuck in between us.

"What's the matter, Anna?" Fabrizio was keeping an eye on me.

"Nothing."

"I know what it is." Simone made me feel uncomfortable. After that one time we had gone out together, I had always avoided him and he never missed a chance to needle me.

"You need someone to smother you with love. Isn't that so?" He took my chin between his fingers.

"Let me be!" I recoiled with a jerk. I felt a kind of repulsion for this guy even though he was so handsome.

"You'd like that, eh Simo? But she doesn't have such ordinary tastes." Joking, but not too much, Fabrizio had come to my defense—my guardian angel. I peeked at Marco—we were separated by only a few feet—yet he was inaccessible. He hadn't noticed a thing because he was flirting with Janina, a South American model. Irritated, I immediately stopped looking at him. I knew he was playing cat and mouse. He had raised a wall between us and I was trying to knock it down, one piece at a time, while he was mending it with tenacity and determination. But I wasn't going to give up.

For Italy v Germany we got organized ahead of time; the game was so important that we Italians and a few other sympathizers took a few hours off work. We booked a table at Serafina. The place was packed and the tension sky-high. Even though there were over twenty of us, this time I managed to get a seat next to Marco.

97

"Annina," he wove his fingers into mine and held our arms up high. "I have a feeling that this time we're going to screw the Krauts. Come on, you'll bring us luck." The mere contact of our hands, our nearness, gave me an injection of positive energy. I was excited, but not the way everyone else was, about the semifinal; the game I was playing was another thing altogether. There was a lot of noise, and it was almost impossible to follow conversations.

Opposite me, Zoe was trying to tell me something, she accentuated her lip movements, "Well, have you pulled it off?" She nodded toward Marco. "Did you get him?" She signed off with a strange grimace, a wry face. I felt myself blushing and gave her a dirty look.

"Are you hot?" Marco asked.

"Yes." I floundered around looking for an answer. "I feel like I'm in my local dry cleaners. They live enveloped in steam. It's the same here."

"You're right. Something's wrong with the air con." In fact, others were complaining too. The women had taken off jackets and sweaters, and some were fidgeting and waving napkins. A couple had taken out fans.

"I'll go ask." Marco was already on his feet, heading for the bar. He was moving away from me on account of a stupid breakdown. There, he was out of my reach once more.

"I'm sweating. It's terrible." Janina had planted her elbows on the table and was delicately pressing a Kleenex on her brow and cheeks. Unfortunately she was still fantastically beautiful even with slightly translucent skin, which made her even more sensual.

"Oh god, this was all we needed." Zoe seemed fresh as a daisy, perhaps the only one in there who wasn't sweating.

"It's not that bad." I tried to be accommodating. "It's been off for less than ten minutes."

"With all these people...Look at their faces."

Zoe set to rummaging in her bag. "If they don't fix it right now I'm going back to the office."

"What about the game?"

"I couldn't care less. Anyway, I don't see any Marco for me here." She smiled as she ran her index and middle fingers across her red lips.

Now everyone was agitated because of the heat. I thought they were laying it on thick; in Italy no one would have got so worked up. But I had learned that in New York having the air conditioning set to icy cold was a religion. Various people had stood up, but without leaving their tables, and were craning their necks in a bid to catch an explanation and, above all, to find out how long it might take for the problem to be fixed. The general murmur had now become a protest movement. I remained seated, dripping, a rivulet of sweat running down between my breasts, and I could feel my hair wet at the back of my neck. I felt dizzy. I was aware that there was a rather strained little smile on my face, which denoted a certain discomfort, albeit not a serious one. Of course, it wasn't the heat that was making me feel ill so much as the loss of hope that assailed me every now and then. I despaired of getting anywhere with Marco. From time to time I tried to restrain my obsession about that love. I didn't understand that I should have been more forgiving toward myself and plead all the mitigating circumstances of a young girl on her first true love.

I was lost, lost. LOST.

"Just one minute and everything's gonna be fine, folks," a waiter announced in a booming voice.

"No worries." Marco was sitting beside me once more. "Everything's fixed. It was only..." The temperature in the room was already falling, which was met with little cries of satisfaction. A few minutes later the climate resembled that of the vegetable bin in the fridge. The incident was forgotten and the problem solved moments before the game was due to begin.

"Right, here we go," someone said and there was an intermittent buzz, while some coarse yelling and even a trumpet increased the confusion. The players had come on to the field. Fabrizio was on his feet, gazing at the screen and casting truculent looks all around. He looked down on us with the air of a rabble-rouser, as if the national team were his private property.

"Will you look at them? You see how jumpy they are?" Zoe nodded in the direction of the men, with that air of superiority that only she had. I adored her for that, but others disliked her. Her advantage, the thing that several people detested her for, was the innate class that distinguished her in any situation. She wasn't like anyone else, she didn't have to be.

"The anthem, the anthem..." The word *anthem* spread like a chant all around the room. When the players began to sing, many joined in the chorus, subdued at first then louder. Eyes were shining, some even moist; some of the Italians' chins were trembling a bit. It was one of those moments in which people put aside bad feelings and rivalries, jealousies, dislikes, and suspicions and everyone is a brother, even strangers, everyone is immersed in a pool of nostalgia in which fuzzy images of mamma, pizza, and the hometown stadium float to the surface.

Marco squeezed my hand, without looking at me. He was concentrating on the song. When the last notes died away he loosened his grip and I noticed he was doing the same thing with Janina. He had held her hand, too. And I who didn't think I had reached the finish line, but thought that I had at least scored a point...Instead, my goal had been disallowed.

I was tired. One minute I felt great, as if in heaven, the next I was down. It was a seesaw I couldn't take for much longer.

The game began, and I pretended to watch the plays while, impermeable to the hubbub, I was thinking, 'What is this thing that drives me toward a man who I basically don't know? I have always been rational. If love gives me no relief, then it's better to give up.'

My thoughts ebbed and flowed, like waves.

The others were following the plays, supportive in body and soul. With *hearts swelling with pride*, to quote the authors of certain articles that fit all occasions. The fact is we're all good Italians, and just like the natives of other nations, we belong to a great country that, if the team wins, will agree about everything for a few days.

Marco turned toward me again, and I sketched a smile that changed into a horrible grimace.

"You know, Anna, I feel this is the most important game of my life." He reached out a hand to move aside the hair covering my eyes. I had shaken it forward, to hide myself, but he couldn't know that. Anyway, that's exactly what he said, "the most important game." We stared at each other for a moment, then his attention was attracted by an offside decision. Like the others, I too was yelling encouragement or swelling the ohhhs of disappointment when a play went badly, yet I wasn't there; I was chewing over his words and the tone he had used. I sat there like a dummy for the entire second half.

When extra time began and Grosso scored, the place went crazy. The clamor, the shouting, struck me like a fist. In a corner there was a table with five or six Germans. They were dumbstruck, with gray faces and clenched jaws. The closing minutes were all action, then Grosso and Del Piero worked the miracle and drew us into a joyous madhouse.

Marco hugged me tight. It wasn't an embrace between fans, well maybe it was at first, but then something melted between us. He pushed me away, only a little, then came closer and kissed me. A real kiss, which swept away the doubts of reason.

All around us it was chaos. Immediately afterward we went out in the street to go to Little Italy. We held hands and then, in the midst of the celebrations, we had to let go. A mass of fans came between us, our fingers slipped out of a clasp that had become too long, we lost our grip and in the hand of one there remained only momentarily the form of the other's.

At the end of the street I lost sight of Marco, swallowed up by the vortex of people gone crazy, their faces painted with the colors of the Italian flag. Many of them were wearing the team's shirts and chanting over and over *I-ta-lia, I-ta-lia*, waving their arms in the air. Loudspeakers emitted songs that resounded over a medley of other sounds that alternately drowned each other out, depending on the acoustics and the angle you were listening from. In general, the notes overlapped one another in a musical fantasia dominated by the ubiquitous hit song composed for the Italian World Cup campaign.

I caught up with Marco again later, or at least I thought I was about to catch up with him. I noticed his gaze: he was looking at me amongst all the people, but got pushed forward. He disappeared among the crowd, together with the others in our party. I was happy all the same—he had kissed me. A passionate kiss that had had great significance.

A beginning. Yes, our story had begun.

Later, I saw Fabrizio's head emerge from the flamboyant crush of fans. He raised his arm, yelling something. I couldn't hear him, the din was like a waterfall, but amplified. At a certain point I realized that Fabrizio was pointing to something or someone behind me. Then he, too, vanished in the torrent, leaving me with a hand gesture with thumb and index finger joined: okay. Alone in that joyous chaos, I didn't feel entirely easy, even though it was daytime. I turned around and saw Simone a few yards away. He was right behind me in a flash.

"Fabrizio spotted you." I was relieved by that encounter.

"Yes," he cried. "Are you so radiant because of the team? I didn't take you for much of a fan." He took me by the arm and tried to lead me to the side of the street, toward the sidewalk, on the edge of the heart of the party.

I realized that my happiness must have been as evident as it was unashamed. "Heck, Italy won. Are you kidding?" I lied brazenly. I was so happy about Marco's kiss that I felt moved.

Simone didn't notice. "Yeees," he cried. "Today is our day. A great day for Italyyyy." He wasn't saying that to me, he was singing it to the world and in that moment all of us there were singing the same song. He looked beatific, like a little boy. We ended up swallowed by a bunch of people who had improvised a kind of tarantella. There wasn't much room, yet they had managed to divide into three couples. They were holding each other by the arm and facing one another. Someone had gotten hold of castanets and tambourines, from god knows where, and the couples, dancing backward and forward, spun and reeled and changed partners.

Simone took my arm and we took to the improvised dance floor. Somehow or other we joined the dancers, staggering more than dancing. Anyway, I didn't even know the steps and my partner was pretty clumsy too, but it was fine like that. The enthusiasm for Italy's win transcended any reasoning. It was pure happiness allied to a feeling of power, the same thing you feel when you first ride a wave on a surfboard.

"Come on." Simone was pulling me in another direction. "We have to celebrate properly."

"What do you think we're doing?" I was laughing. I felt light and I didn't even notice the knocks delivered by knees and elbows, hips and heads, which I couldn't dodge as I cut through the crowd behind Simone. Luckily my bag was slung over my shoulder and I kept one hand firmly over the clasp.

"Come on," Simone repeated. "Let's take a breather." He was leaning against the window of a restaurant shaded by large red, white and green awnings. We were surrounded by the crowd, but a curve in the wall gave us a respite from the unstoppable wild exultation of our compatriots.

"You're a real hottie, Anna. You know that?" His voice, hoarse and a bit slurred, prompted me to slip to one side to get away from him, but it was useless. Now Simone had me pressed up against the window that guarded a collection of improbable pizzas. His expression had changed, his face too near, the smell of smoke mixed with that of alcohol. I recognized the same wolfish look I had glimpsed for a moment on the bridge on the evening of our date.

I was annoyed, but I didn't feel in danger among all those people. I limited myself to scolding him. "Forget it." I tried to wriggle free and he grabbed my arm, twisting it behind my back.

"Don't be an idiot. We're here to celebrate." I looked around—no one was paying any attention to us.

"Yes, cutie. We're here to do just that." His face had become hard, his jaw clenched, his eyes slits. He tilted his head back. I thought he wanted to size me up, gauge how far he could go in making a pass at me. But he had been drinking, maybe he was even high on coke. I wasn't really worried yet, I was sure I could handle the situation. At least for the time being.

"Cut it out, Simone. Quit it. This isn't like you. You're drunk. That's enough now." My tone was confident, I was speaking loudly to carry over the noise of the crowd and the music, but I wasn't yelling yet.

"Come on, let's find a place and…I'll make you feel something that'll make you want to…" He grabbed my arm and was pulling me beyond the perimeter of the window while he caressed my neck with his other hand and his fingers strayed as far as the swell of my breasts. I tried to free my wrist from his grip but failed. Suddenly I lost it, anger making me stronger. "Idiot!" I yelled at the top of my voice. A few people around us realized that we weren't celebrating Italy's victory. A group of three guys looked at us in puzzlement. One of them, thickset, with bushy eyebrows, moved to my side without saying a word. In his eyes I read the determination of a savior.

"Let me go. Let go of my wrist," I yelled again, this time turning toward the guy. I would never have hoped for it, but Simone's expression changed to a stunned look, then he released me. I turned around and entered the embrace of the crowd, without a backward glance.

I took the subway and came back up in my neighborhood, where there was no reason for manifestations of joy for Italy's victory. I walked slowly along the stretch of road between there and my place, then I sped up; every now and then I began to skip and I even attempted a sideways gallop, the way little kids do when they're playing in a group. Waves of anger and disgust alternated with moments of exultation. The latter were by far the most prevalent, thanks to the memory of Marco's kiss. The round of applause given by a group of kids in front of the bookstore brought me back to the present.

The next day I almost flew to the office. I came out of the elevator and glimpsed Marco at the end of the corridor. He was in shape, looking rested, yet I figured he had celebrated Italy's win into the small hours of the night. I was wearing a new white dress with thin shoulder straps, on top of which I had a peach colored linen jacket. I was a bit agitated; I had to control myself in order to seem calm, back in the habitual friendly relationship between colleagues. I was expecting to meet a knowing glance, some words left hanging in the air that only I could interpret. Instead, all I got was the usual polite smile that demolished all my certainties and ruined my mood. I kept telling myself that Marco behaved that way to avoid gossip in the office, but there was no excuse for this display of indifference. I caught his sidelong look as he was smiling at a new intern who had just arrived, and I headed in his direction, determined to feign detachment. I realized immediately that he was enraptured by something completely different.

"What a day." Marco was waving his hands in excitement. "It really was the greatest game I've ever seen. It must have been something in Italy! I really would have liked to be there, in my country. To see it with my friends..." He was daydreaming and gesticulating, running the risk of spilling the glass of water in his hand. He was a prey to an attack of joyful melancholy.

'Idiot, don't you remember that you kissed me?' I thought. I was still full of expectation for a budding love affair. I was shaken and my heart was broken because our first kiss counted less than two goals.

106

Marco carried on commentating on the game, waving his arms and acting out the plays. The story had become a collective narrative, given that we had been joined by other colleagues. All men engaged in one of their favorite rituals: running through the story of the game of the century. I wanted to hurt Marco, or at least spoil his fun. "But you dumped me in the middle of that madhouse and you didn't even worry about what might have happened to me," I whispered sourly in his ear. He instantly broke off his monologue and moved toward me, leaving the group.

"Why? Did something happen to you?"

"Yes." I was vexed. We had moved into a side corridor to let others pass, on their way for a coffee break.

"What happened?" Now I had his complete attention. I took my time. I was placated by the crease that had appeared on his forehead. For me.

"Simone. After we lost sight of each other in the crowd, he showed up."

"And then?"

"Nothing. You know what Simone's like when he gets started." I felt uncomfortable. I lowered my voice and Marco came closer. "He bothered me." I spilled the beans and felt better.

"What happened? What did he do to you?" He had paled and I was enjoying that.

"Nothing happened. He bothered me. He went too far." I didn't feel like going into detail. "I don't like Simone," I concluded.

"I want you to tell me everything." Marco looked at his watch: "I have to go now. We'll talk about this later, after work." His handsome face widened into a smile that was a caress. He brushed my hand, deliberately, and slipped along the corridor toward his office.

# 11
## VENDETTA

I was furious, but I didn't want Anna to notice. I had lost her in the sea of people. I had allowed her to fall behind, to slip away, while I was struggling to follow Janina.

What a shit Simone had been.

What a shit I had been.

I had never liked Simone. A guy who enjoyed the legend of New York on Daddy's money. Money that he squandered. The fact that he had expensive vices was common knowledge. God. What if apart from behaving like an idiot he had tried to...

I remembered well the kiss Anna and I had shared the evening before. It had started as one of those kisses people give in a moment of revelry, but it ended as something more than that.

She had put her heart into it and I liked it.

As soon as I got back to the office, I checked Rosario's diary, which was full of out-of-office appointments. So I was going to be alone that afternoon. 'Good,' I thought. 'I have to think about how to manage things with Simone, and with Anna, too.'

There could be nothing between us. As far as I was concerned, the beginning of any kind of relationship with an intern was impossible. She would have to live with that. Yet, right there, sitting at my desk in front of the computer, I was eventually forced to admit to myself that I was interested in the Venetian girl.

Damn. The conditions were all wrong.

No way. I put a stop to it.

I told myself this colossal falsehood in complete ill faith. She, the tiramisu girl with the honest face, whose skin was the scent of home, was stuck in my head like a nail. I could no longer think rationally. To tell the truth I felt confused, uncomfortable and irritated.

I had to relax and manage the situation. Or better, put the girl aside; anyway, she was hardly going to stay here forever. Besides, I was planning to go back to Italy for ten days for my brother's wedding. I would be leaving soon and a change of scene would do me good.

But the business with Simone had to be cleared up.

It was almost seven when I went to take a peek in Anna's office. The workstations near hers were deserted. She was putting on lipstick, a crimson mark on the pale face reflected slantwise on the computer screen.

"Come on. Let's go drink something and you can tell me what happened with Simone."

Anna had spun around, embarrassed. She shrugged and lowered her head. Then she gave me a smile. I have a clear memory of the sequence of her movements. There was no seductive intent, she was confused and happy at the same time, and for that very reason she was even more attractive.

"Fantastic. Putting on lipstick is a very private thing. Don't you know that?"

"No, given that you're doing it here instead of the ladies' room." We both laughed.

We headed off side by side along the corridor toward the el-evators. There was something wrong, and that was due to me. I was uncomfortable because I felt too much ease with Anna. I couldn't be indifferent to her even though I tried not to think about her. Perhaps it was too late and I had to resign myself to the fact that by now I was caught in the net of an extraordinary infatuation. The very situation I wanted to avoid at all costs.

I remained silent as the cabin took us down and she didn't say a word either. We crossed the lobby without so much as exchanging a glance.

"Where are we going?" Anna said, leaning out of the door. Now she was hesitant.

"Let's go to the 230. Do you remember it? We went there for the Valentino midsummer party. It's not very far away." I took her arm and we threaded our way into the crowd.

"Okay." Now she was smiling, relaxed. "Let's walk, that way we can chat for a while." But she remained silent almost all the way. Every so often she glanced at me—maybe she wanted to tell me something. I limited myself to a few words about the surroundings. I preferred to wait until we were sit-ting in the bar before she told me her story.

We chose a secluded table, where the background noise produced by the other clients was muffled and that was lucky because more and more people kept arriving. She began to tell me something about the office, and I nodded without lis-tening. I liked to observe her as she moved, her hands as they played their part in the telling of the story, her eyes and mouth as they interpreted the content of the conversation. I realized that, despite my resolutions, I was looking at the pe-tite Venetian girl in a way different than the way I looked at other women who attracted me. I liked all of her, inside and out. She was a kind of magnet.

"You seem fresh as a daisy. How do you do it?" I asked her.

"I know. It's always been this way. Nobody notices even if I'm dying before their very eyes. A gift of nature, I think." Now she was agitated again. She was toying with the paper napkin, folding it over and over until it was reduced to the size of a postage stamp. We ordered iced coffee and water with ice.

"Well, I'm totally pooped."

"What does that mean?" I noticed that her dark eyes got even bigger when she was asking someone a question.

"It just means I'm tired out, exhausted."

"I'm sorry," she said, with a hint of regret. "Listen, what happened with Simone isn't that important. It's not worth..."

"No." I raised my hand imperiously. "We must talk about it, and how! I just need a drink right now. Don't worry." I called over a waiter and ordered a margarita. Anna didn't want anything.

"So, tell me about it," I invited her.

"I don't know..." She hesitated, uncomfortable. She blushed. After a long pause she went on, "You know that one evening I went out with Simone? Only the one time, and that was enough for me. Among other things I found out that... No, this doesn't come into it, but it's something that bothered me." She was ill at ease again and maybe that's why she had huddled down in her seat. She seemed more delicate.

"We all know he does cocaine big time," I said to relieve the tension. "Sometimes we even talked to him about it. He's let it go way too far, he just can't leave it alone. He's an idiot."

"Well, I didn't know that you..." She was relieved at not having revealed anything new.

"Forget it. Tell me what happened."

"It's not worth it. It was a silly thing. I shouldn't have said anything to you. In reality nothing happened."

"Hold on, did Simone bother you, yes or no?"

"I don't want to make a big deal of it." She slipped two fingers into my glass, took an ice cube and ran it over her lips. She didn't realize what she was doing.

"I want to know. Did you bump into him by chance? Or did you get the feeling he had followed you on purpose?"

"No, I don't believe so. I think he found himself near me so...You know, in that crowd...it wasn't easy to follow someone."

"And then?"

"Nothing. I tried to follow you but I lost you. I found myself near Simone. We were celebrating like everyone else. We danced the tarantella in the middle of the street and until then it had been fun." At that point Anna stopped talking and concentrated her attention on the people at the next table, two guys and a girl who looked as if they had come out of a Dolce & Gabbana ad. I didn't let myself be distracted and brought her back to our present.

"I bet this is where we get to the most interesting part. Right, Anna?"

"Simone paid me a few compliments. I realized he was drunk. I hate people calling me a 'hottie.' We stopped at the side of the street and he grabbed my wrist. He wouldn't let me go," She ended hastily.

"And then what happened?"

She looked at me as if I were stupid. "What happened was he let me go and I went away. That's it. Now do you see that it was no big deal? Anyway, there's no way he'll be able to bother me again."

"That's for sure!" I took her hand and squeezed it. I would have like to spend the rest of the evening with her, but instead I said goodbye and left. I couldn't wait to sort this matter out.

***

Things ended badly with Simone. I sent him a message on a pretext, telling him to come see me. No doubt he understood straight off where I intended to go with this. I had just got back home when I heard the door handle turn.

"Here I am." Simone came in without knocking and closed the door behind him. He was wearing a mocking smile, ripped jeans and a gray T-shirt with 'I'm a Mommy's Boy' written on it in Italian. I said nothing.

"Here I am," he repeated, with the hoarse voice he got when he'd just had a snort. "Bet you I can guess what you want to talk to me about?" He sat down on a chair and took out his cigarettes.

"That means you have a guilty conscience." I felt like busting him in the mouth, but I decided to restrain my anger. I was going to ask him for an explanation, and I forced myself to have a calm but resolute talk with him. No way he was going to approach Anna again.

"The little slut is a tease," he said. "I hope she gives it to you at least." The shit gave a vulgar laugh and my fist connected squarely with his jaw and slid up toward his forehead. He wasn't expecting it, a sign that he didn't know me at all. He went staggering backward and crashed into the bureau and stayed there for a while, stunned. Blood came from his nose and lip. I thought it was all over, but instead he charged me with his head down. I moved, but couldn't avoid him altogether because the table blocked my escape route; his head hit me in the chest, causing me to lose my balance and fall to the floor. Now Simone had straightened up, his face smeared with blood as he prepared to kick me in the side. Instinctively I extended my foot and hit him in the groin, making him double up and gasp.

His blood dripped onto my shirt. I got back on my feet quickly—the fight was over. "Don't try that ever again. Leave Anna alone." He was panting as he dabbed at his face with one hand. I shoved him toward the door, stooped as he was.

"You can keep your Anna. She's hooked you, eh. You're hot for her. Fuck, my nose is swelling up, you shit!" Simone was looking around for something. Maybe he hoped I would be moved to pity and give him some ice. My only response was to give him a final backhand and throw open the door. He stumbled out, crashing into Pepita.

"*Ahi Dios! Qué pasa niños?*" she cried. I slammed the door shut without a word. I didn't want to see anyone; I needed to calm down.

Had I gone too far with Simone? No. He needed a lesson. He had disrespected Anna.

Anna.

It was impossible to ignore her, she always popped up again; at the coffee machine in the office, or crossing the corridor from where her voice would come to me, or diving into the elevator, where I was, a split second before the doors closed. In the evenings, when a group of us went out, her eyes would follow me. She observed my every move even when she wasn't looking, I felt it. And when she wasn't around, every so often she would sneak into my head.

What an idiot Simone was. But now he would leave Anna in peace. I started to strip off; I needed a shower. The hot water ran over me and I tilted my head back to get the jet right in my face, a habit I had had since I was a kid. In a few days' time I would be back home for Matteo's wedding.

Home was in Fano, a town on the coast, a detached house on two floors with a small yard that I used to think was enormous.

The garage where I used to keep my bicycle, a Bianchi, and where I still parked my mint green Vespa, an original 1962 model I had bought from a friend. From the garage you accessed the laundry room. Every time I went back home it was if I could see my mom bent over doing laundry when I, homework assignments done, would run downstairs, "Mom, I'm done. I'm taking my bicycle down to the sports field." She would turn around with a smile and nod to me that I could go. She didn't stop scrubbing the laundry with the hard brush even for a moment.

Then one day she went out shopping and never came back home. She was hit by a truck, like the one my father drove.

For years no other woman entered our house, until Matteo's fiancée, Sofia, came along.

And now my brother was marrying her.

I was happy for him. For us. I liked Sofia. The second woman in our family of men only. She had appeared one day, without any warning. The first thing I knew about her was her voice.

"May I come in?" She had opened the door that, still from the garage, led to the stairs and the kitchen. She was blonde with big eyes and an embarrassed smile. At that time I was just a kid, maybe not even eighteen. At first I felt shy, but it wasn't long before a genuine liking grew up between us. From then on she became my reference point, my friend, discreet and always present. My confidante, too.

I turned the faucet and the hot water became icy. I turned it off immediately, shivering. For a moment Anna's face was superimposed over Sofia's. I had to clear my mind. I put on my bathrobe and wiped the steam off the mirror with the palm of my hand. The scuffle with Simone hadn't left any marks on my face. Besides, he had gotten the worst of it. I was going to take a stroll outside, by myself, just to take my mind off things and let my anger subside.

# 12
## ON THE ROLLER COASTER

A handshake, a brotherly affection. We had spent almost two hours alone together chatting at the table and, when we left, Marco said goodbye with a kiss on the cheek.

I felt incredibly angry, but cooled off during the journey home on the subway. Maybe he thought I was going to wait forever? This was replaced by an acute feeling of sadness, a pang in the middle of my chest that never left me as I dragged myself all the way home. Luckily Asena was out; I needed to be alone for a while.

Marco was important, Marco was love. Maybe, just maybe, a common destiny was in store for us. But he wasn't giving an inch and stubbornly kept me at a distance.

"So leave me in peace," I hissed in front of the bathroom mirror as I sprinkled my wrists and temples with cold water. Since I had met him my thoughts were no longer clear—I was confused, as if my head was wrapped in tight gauze bandages that didn't let my thoughts expand, or reach out in other directions. My mind was a funnel that converged on Marco. In my dreams I entered dark, scary tunnels and at the end he was always there, Marco, my knight in shining armor.

In reality, the rare occasions in which I saw a few glimpses of familiarity open up between us did not make up for the periods of despondency. I was almost getting used to the negative moments while happiness...well, that had become an abstract concept, a goal that perhaps I was going to have to set aside.

Later on I had tried to talk about this with Asena, but her mind was elsewhere. She had spent the entire day going around the stores, absorbed in her wedding preparations. I needed to confide in someone I trusted and decided to call Beatrice, in Italy.

"Well, what do you expect? You tell me he's good looking, intelligent and on his way up. He probably has other goals." Bea's response was sour in the extreme.

"But he likes me, I'm sure."

"My dear girl, you're fantasizing. Come back to planet Earth."

"But I'm sure..." Sitting on the bed with my legs crossed, I was wringing the hem of the sheet.

"Like that time in Chile, with that guy with the absurd name, Rodrigo? Listen to me, Anna. Don't even think about it." I didn't understand why Bea was being so negative and above all why she was using that cutting tone of voice. Did she perhaps enjoy hurting me? I started to sniff, and I felt like crying. As a matter of fact, the tears were already running down and wetting the neck of my blouse. I started to undress as I listened.

"Besides, look at it from another point of view. Judging by what you tell me he'll probably stay there. Right?" Bea continued.

"He has a really good job. He's smart and he's destined to go far. I really don't think he'll go back to Italy." I got a hold of myself and began to dry my face with the hem of my T-shirt.

"Exactly. You come from the country, from the Veneto. You don't come into things at all. He's on another planet. We can't have any doings with people like that. Such circles are not for us." I heard a sound like a breath being sucked in. I figured she was smoking in that theatrical way of hers. All her friends made fun of her for that.

"You're wrong. We're all equal here. I like it fine in New York." I got up and paced up and down in the cramped space available to me. I realized I was arguing with Bea. Why did she always have to run down everything I did? She was jealous and wanted to humiliate me.

"I'm off to bed now. It's night here." I ended the call quickly, rudely. She had no right to bring me down.

"Don't think about him anymore. He's not for people like us," she recited as I was searching for something to say before putting down the phone. She had the power to psych me out, to undermine my self-esteem and consequently, my confidence. She always said 'us.' But I was Anna and I was working in New York. She, Bea, was buried in an anonymous town dreaming of a man who would marry her and keep her at home away from a clerical job she didn't like. She could go to hell.

"Ciao. And don't fool yourself, you silly thing. Certain things don't happen to us, you know that." But I didn't know that and it wasn't necessarily so. In that moment I was tempted to break off with my best friend forever. I didn't say anything to her, I simply put down the phone. The road to happiness was difficult and tough. I would go far.

I wasn't Bea, I was Anna.

At lunchtime the next day I was leaving the office when Fabrizio ran up to me. "Anna, wait up. Do you know what happened between Marco and Simone?" he asked me point blank. "Don't play dumb. Yesterday evening they had a furious bust up. Pepita told me, the poor thing. She was scared to death."

"I don't know anything about this..." I was even more shocked than he.

"You don't mind if I come with you, do you?" he asked sardonically.

"Given that we do that every day..."

"Yes, like good friends. But now I'm not so sure anymore. If you lot don't take me into your confidence, I don't know what to think." He squinted against the sunlight.

I didn't answer him right away. We headed toward Bryant Park, then I muttered, "Was it a bad bust up?"

"Well, if *you* don't know what happened...? So?" Fabrizio was pressing me even with his gaze.

"Why didn't you ask Marco?"

"I didn't see him. He left very early. I think he had to go to Chicago with Rosario."

"So where were you yesterday? What does Pepita have to do with it?" I stopped in the middle of the sidewalk. Fabri took my arm and obliged me to fall in with the pace of the crowd, which was rather substantial at that time of day.

"She lives there, remember. She's the landlady. I missed the show because I wasn't there. I went off to work late and then I had an appointment with the Jamaican dentist, who tortured me in the bargain."

"I'm sorry. How are you feeling now?"

"Anna, don't play games. Forget about me. I want to know what happened. Pepita said she heard Marco shouting your name. She said those two came to blows."

"Over me? I can't believe it." I couldn't help smiling.

"Not over me, for sure. Come on, cut it out. I'm getting mad, really." In the meantime, we had come to our favorite bench, but it was taken by two girls with skates on their feet. They were on their lunch break, too.

"Come on, Fabri. Let's find a place and you can tell me what you've found out."

"You tell me what *you* know. I'm your best friend and you won't tell me anything?" Fabrizio was staring at me with bulging eyes, offended at being kept in the dark about something he thought concerned him.

We sat down and I spilled the beans to him. Then I took out my bottle of mineral water and sipped at it while Fabrizio pensively chewed on his sandwich. We remained in silence, surrounded by the sounds of the park, which was lively with lots of people at that hour. Some were strolling, others stretched out on the grass enjoying the sunshine, still others playing with their dogs. Some were reading, others were absorbed in chess games, two groups of elderly people were playing bocce, while others were watching workers setting up the screen for the movie scheduled to play that evening. The week before, I had seen *La Dolce Vita*. It had been thrilling to watch Marcello and Anna flirting, with the lights of Times Square in the background. The tables of the bars on the edge of the square were full to overflowing with colorful humanity. I, instead, felt like a fish out of water. As always in those days, I missed Marco, who wasn't even mine. At least, not for the time being.

"Don't give up, Anna!" Fabrizio jumped to his feet and brushed the crumbs off his shirt. He took his jacket from the back of the bench and flipped it over his shoulder. I took my bag and the container with the remains of my lunch, then got up with scant enthusiasm.

"Wake up, Anna." He was looking at me and laughing. "It's in the bag, don't you see?"

"Who? What?"

"Marco."

"You're wrong. I mean nothing to him. He's not interested in me and he doesn't want me."

"Oh, women." He turned around, still laughing. "Talk about the sixth sense! You haven't understood a thing. Come on, it's late. Race you to the office?" He began to run, hooting with laughter, but the wall of people forced him to slow down until he dropped down to a walk.

I followed him against my will. I was walking in a sort of dream, bumping into the people coming the other way. I didn't see them, yet there would have been a lot to see, as always in New York. There were whites, blacks, and Asians of all different shades, South Americans, Latinos...They were young and old and the middle-aged, a few kids and toddlers with mothers or nannies. The older ones were at school. The style of their clothing was like an infinite collection, yet... Yet every tall, slim man had Marco's features, and all the rest were faceless.

There was no way I could stop thinking about him, I just couldn't, nor did I want to.

I wasn't yet entirely sure that Marco returned my feelings. There certainly was some interest, or maybe...After all, he had gone so far as to fight for me. I was certainly in this thing, I had fallen into a love that enveloped me like molasses and there was no way out.

A girl skating in the opposite direction lurched into me heavily and I nearly fell. The unexpected event broke the spell I was under.

"Fabri, wait up." I sprinted to catch up with him. I slipped my arm under his and gripped his wrist tightly. Laughing, he looked at me in surprise.

"Yes, you're right," I said, quickening my pace and dragging him close to me. "I'm going to win this challenge, you'll see. Marco has no escape. I want to trust you."

The background noise of cars, the flashing lights of the signs that broke the tunnel of shadow cast by the skyscrapers all along the road, the segment of sky looming overhead, colored with a special blue—everything contributed to reinforcing the impression that the city was my close friend. By now I belonged to it. Perhaps I might spend my life here, with Marco.

"And you do right," Fabri said. By that time we had reached the entrance to the office building. "Come on. If you don't hurry we'll be late and then it'll be Valentino who doesn't trust us anymore and we'll be sent home before time." Fabri laughed as he gave me a gentle shake, freeing his arm from my grip. "So, you're convinced? Will you go ahead?" he added, entering before me.

"I'm not backing out. I want Marco." God knows why, but as I said that I got a lump in my throat.

"Good girl, Anna. That's the way to go. But now let's get back to work." Fabrizio dragged me into the lobby, then into the elevator before leading me all the way to my office. "Remember that we're going out tomorrow. I figure that Simone won't be joining us. It'll be just us three. Make yourself look nice." He patted me on the cheek. "But what am I saying? You hardly need to do that."

For the rest of the afternoon I got nothing done.

That evening after work, I boarded the subway with a naïve idea in mind—I would weave around Marco a web of affections and more or less discreet pampering, in which he would be hopelessly snared. For a start, before going home I popped into the Chinese deli and bought three slabs of hazelnut chocolate that I then broke up into big coarse chunks on the kitchen table. I arranged the butchered pieces of chocolate on a little serving dish with a floral pattern and wrapped the whole thing in white gift paper. I secured the package with a king-sized bright yellow bow.

A couple of hours later, in bed, I drifted off to sleep looking forward to the effect the surprise would have on Marco the next morning. "For you. I spent the entire evening in the kitchen." I would accompany the gift with one of my most ardent smiles. He would look at me in amazement, munching on the chocolate as a piece of hazelnut got trapped between his teeth.

"That's so good. You have a real talent, Anna."

"Eh, call me Anna of the miracles." I would welcome his loving gaze.

That was my fantasy for that evening.

The next morning in the office, Marco wanted to share my gift with Rosario, Fabrizio and a few others. It was much appreciated and no one doubted my skills as a confectioner, but Marco's reaction was less romantic than expected. He mumbled his thanks and then added, "I'll call the others. This is too much for just me."

We were deadlocked, and I had little time. I knew that he was due to leave for Italy very soon to be at his brother's wedding. What's more, my internship was almost at an end. I had to speed things up. Deciding to throw all caution to the winds, I took advantage of the lunch break to furtively slip a letter, a kind of declaration, into the top drawer of his desk. The missive was addressed *To my dear Marco*.

By chance I had occasion to observe his reaction when he found it. I saw him open the drawer and look at the envelope; there was no doubt he understood that I had sent it. He looked around and spotted me, midway along the corridor. All the same, with an indifferent air, he slipped the letter beneath some other papers without opening it, and then he closed his office door. I could only hope that once he was alone he would pick it up again and devour the contents.

I was disheartened.

I didn't even feel like going out that evening with him and Fabrizio.

# 13
## The Letter

"My dear Marco, there's no way you can escape our Anna." Fabrizio gave a knowing smile.

"Shit, now you're in this too? It's time to cut it out," I exploded.

"Look, you're in it up to your neck by now. And you know it. This thing with the Venetian, as you call her, is a big deal, not just nothing."

"Listen, do me a favor—get to work." I was exasperated by Anna's letter. I wasn't mad at her, quite the contrary. She had shown a lot of guts by declaring herself. The problem lay with me. I still couldn't define how I felt. It was difficult to say because it was no small matter.

I was sure that if I let instinct take over I would find myself in a minefield. I would have to give up the idea of continuing on along my path the way I had imagined it—mine was a life mostly planned out, which was why I was careful to avoid running into distractions, or worse, love affairs. Sure, Fabri would say I was thinking like an old man and that in any case, wrong moves elude all logic. Things happen and that's that.

But I kept on thinking, with a feeling of irritation, that Anna was a magnet to be avoided. Someone once said, 'The heart has its reasons of which reason knows nothing.' Good grief, now I was pulling out sayings from Sweetheart candies. Anna had already begun to be bad for me.

I had to be practical—the only path to follow was that of reason, the heart only creates confusion.

"I'm off. I'll see you this evening. A night out for three, remember?" Fabrizio's tone was mischievous. "I might be a tad late, I have another session with the dentist. Now, in my absence make sure you don't get into any fights or get engaged." He disappeared down the corridor.

Embarking on a serious love affair was out of the question, absolutely against my principles. I loved order, and Anna was a whirlwind. A relationship with her would involve a series of steps, questions that had very little importance, for me at least, but women cannot live without certain answers: we'll get engaged, we'll live together and get married, then a child or two and a big house...I'd already been there, in Fano. I wasn't going to pay any more dues in New York.

Yet I felt that I missed Anna even though I had never shared anything with her, apart from one kiss. In short, in the end I could try it, just to see how things went. A thing without commitment, then I would leave for Italy, there was the wedding and I would have time to catch my breath.

'If you don't try it you'll never know,' I thought.

Anna would certainly come with us, as we had agreed. She never missed our nights out.

I wanted to see her, but maybe I would continue to steer clear of her. I would pretend not to see her disappointment when I didn't give her so much as a glance. Yes, the best thing for both of us was to find out how it went. Anna, for one night if she agreed, and maybe we would discover that it didn't work the way we thought. It happens. After that, I could get

Anna out of my head, and I would remember her as a brief episode, over by now.

I dressed in a hurry. I hoped she might arrive early. It was a very hot evening. Fabrizio had just come back from the dentist, his cheek a bit swollen and every so often he pressed a hand against it.

"Does it hurt?" I asked him.

He gave a nonchalant shrug: "I'm still under the anesthetic."

"Why don't you put some ice on it? When will the effect wear off?"

"I'll be drunk later on and I won't feel a thing."

We decided to sit on the stoop and wait for Anna to join us. Inside, the old air conditioning system had packed up.

"It is *sobrecalentado*," was Pepita's diagnosis, but she had sounded doubtful.

"Air conditioners don't overheat," Fabrizio laughed, but the idea of sleeping in an oven was a real downer.

"It's too old. It needs changing," I suggested.

"Too many dollars. It can be fixed." Pepita had ended the discussion and we took a seat on the stoop, but there wasn't a breath of air. Yet when Anna got out of the taxi, she brought a gust of freshness. She was wearing a midnight-blue dress, long and feather light, and her bare back wasn't even shiny. Did that girl never sweat?

"Ciao. Will you move over?"

I liked having her close and at the same time it wasn't good. 'Build up the wall. Don't let anyone in, not even Anna. If she gets inside your fortress you're all washed up,' I kept telling myself. In the meantime, I heard her and Fabrizio talking, but I paid no attention to them.

"Anna, you can't go on staying there. It's dangerous. You tell her, too."

"Tell her what?" I replied absently.

"This evening I found out that two homeless people have made their nest in our building. It was by chance, I was taking out the trash and..."

"What chance? Don't you know it's dangerous?" I had immediately pricked up my ears. Anna was capable of getting herself into trouble. First with Simone and now with the homeless. Maybe they were junkies. Everything was happening at once, and Anna was in the middle of it all.

"No way. They're not dangerous. They were going through our trash, they've set up camp in the basement. They're a middle-aged couple. She looks like Annie, the woman with the apple."

"What apple?" Fabrizio stood up and checked his watch.

"The apple in the movie. Do you remember that old movie with Glenn Ford and Bette Davis? I saw it lots of times when I was a kid."[3]

"You can't stay there any longer," I said. "It's not safe." I was tense; I had to persuade her to listen to me.

"Where am I supposed to go? Now that Asena is getting married and I'll have to find a new roommate."

"Come and stay here. At my place. In a couple of days I'm leaving for my brother's wedding. After that, we'll see, anyway, you'll be going back home soon..." Anna said nothing. She stared at me and then, despite the heat, a shiver seemed to run through her.

I realized I had made a mistake, a wrong move that I would perhaps regret. 'But she can hardly stay there alone,' I thought. 'Having her come to my place is the right thing.' In any case, she would go back to Italy when the internship was over; the date would coincide with my return to New York, more or less. Maybe we wouldn't even meet.

"Hey, shall we get a move on? Fabrizio was already standing. Anna and I got up, too, avoiding each other's eyes.

"Let's walk for a bit, then we'll catch a cab on the fly," Anna suggested. And that's what we did. Fabrizio's face began to ache and no one was in a mood to chat. You could sense a tension in the air, similar to the kind before a big storm. All three of us knew that that night was going to mean a lot for Anna and me. Even though he was out of the game, Fabri was definitely rooting for her.

Later, we hailed a cab and I got in beside the driver, away from Anna who sat behind with Fabrizio.

"Two eighty nine 10th Avenue," I said. The car drove off. No one said a word  the whole way.

# 14
# A Night at the Marquee

It was just past two o'clock and the Marquee was packed.

I was dancing listlessly.

Mere gymnastics with no passion.

I observed the colorful group of dancers who swayed and broke up only to re-form like a wave where two seas meet. Music filled every empty space. We were all dancing: Marco, Fabrizio and I. Our movement was underlaid with ill humor. That evening something had broken the harmony that usually marked our nights out. It had infected even Fabrizio, perhaps because of the toothache. In certain moments it was really hard to find enough space to move to the rhythm of the music. Every so often, the network of bodies would thin out and then it was easier to get the bad mood out of my system through movement. I began to feel the effects of the alcohol I had drunk, too much of it. Marco stopped at a tremendous explosion of sound; he was looking at me and moving his lips.

A fish.

The compact wall of sound vibrated, preventing the passage of any human voice. I managed to read his lips.

"Come on. Let's go." Without any warning he grabbed my hand and dragged me along with him to plow through the crush.

In that very moment, the DJs announced that a surprise was on the way. Their metallic voices rose over the din and traveled in an echo effect that reverberated from one side of the nightclub to the other.

I quickened my pace behind Marco. I followed him unthinkingly, too tired or tipsy to think about what was going on.

A moment later we were on the sidewalk of 10th Avenue as a cab drew up right in front of us and disgorged its fares. My head was spinning, I was laughing, but the sound was more like the gurgling of a water fountain and my expression was a bit stupid. Marco had drunk a bit too much too, but was certainly more clearheaded than I.

"Princess..." he ushered me into the cab with a bow.

The car smelled of old grime. I sat down warily, but not before running my hand over the seat. The alcohol-fueled euphoria was dissipating.

"Where are we going?"

"Home. I don't need that shit this evening." Marco slipped into the seat beside me and gave the driver Pepita's address. He took my hand once more as I sank into the creased leather upholstery, split open at several points.

Suddenly I was worried, uneasy.

My nervousness made me wordless.

Why hadn't he given my address, in Queens? When we stayed out late he and Fabrizio always took me home. Maybe his mind was elsewhere and I should have pointed it out, but I said nothing. I didn't utter a word all the way. I looked at him, avoiding his gaze. He looked great, so I had to discard the notion that he was sick.

No point in asking too many questions. I decided that, when the cab reached our destination, I would bid Marco goodnight with a peck on the cheek, as usual, then I would give the driver my address.

That would be the end of it. The evening would end the usual way. I gave a deep sigh. I had tried everything to win Marco.

I was disappointed, but not yet resigned.

I toyed with the idea that he had offered to have me stay in his apartment out of something more than courtesy toward a compatriot.

I was sure he cared about me, but he was stubborn.

He would leave me an empty house.

This time, too, my hopes had been dashed. There was no point in speculating about what *wasn't* happening.

In fact, we were alone in the cab and he didn't say a single word to me.

Everyone in their place.

Yet, I was in New York. Anything could happen here. To others, but not to me. Maybe Bea was right after all.

I hadn't finished that thought when Marco moved his hand next to mine. He began running his long fingers along the inside of my wrist, following the lines of my veins.

A message? A caress. A gesture just for me. Finally.

"Are you tired?"

"No. Not at all." It was hot and the traffic was as heavy as in the daytime. I felt uncomfortable, for no precise reason. Well, there was one—I didn't know what was going on. I thought back on all the things I had come up with in those weeks to please Marco and on the contrasting messages he had sent me. He had never encouraged me. On the contrary, he had done everything to make me understand I should forget it.

And now?

Now he had dragged me into a cab half way through an evening in the Marquee and we were racing toward his place. I didn't have time to follow that reasoning to a conclusion when the car began to slow down. We had arrived.

"Keep the change," Marco said to the driver, then he added, "Would my princess like to get out?"

I hesitated. He noticed and with a smile and a wave of the hand, he renewed the invitation. I slipped out of the cab. Standing on the sidewalk I ran a hand over my dress to smooth out the creases, and my thoughts, too.

Marco had already gone up the few steps to the door and was fiddling with his keys. I went up too and stood behind him.

A breath of hot air made me shudder.

\*\*\*

In the end I decided to follow my instincts. I wanted to understand where an affair with Anna would take me. Watching her dancing in front of me with that disconnected air moved me. She was irresistible and she didn't know it. She played the emancipated woman, she had courted me courageously, she had grit and didn't back down from anything. Would she make a good playmate? All I had to do was take her away from there and find out.

Now or never.

"After you, Princess." Anna wore a strained smile, her eyes timid and curious. She had hesitated before getting into the cab.

Once more I felt torn—I was in the presence of a child. I had second thoughts, I liked her, but I still had time to drop the idea.

Out of caution.

Out of convenience.

136

Because, damn it, I didn't want to get involved with a girl like her.

And now?

What a mistake it had been to bring her home.

What had gotten into me?

All I wanted was to have fun. As Fabrizio had taught me. No commitments, only gymnastics. Just for something to do.

New York was full of gorgeous women you could get into bed with without any problem, setting up an occasional relationship. To spend an hour or two, at most a night, or merely to warm yourself up a bit, with no consequences, just to boost your morale and claim bragging rights.

Anna was different.

Anna.

The idea was beginning to scare me.

No, this was not good.

Stop, Marco! Stop right here while you still can.

I liked Anna, sure.

I was nuts to take her away from the Marquee.

I wanted something real.

But Anna was too much.

She was the kind of girl you have to treat seriously, or not at all. I had understood that from the first moment I saw her. Scrupulous, pretty, stubborn... the frank gaze of a woman looking for the love of her life.

Fabrizio would say: a first-class *Italian* girl.

Too great a luxury for me now.

I wanted something else, fresh meat, sure, but a less noble cut would be better, given the situation.

New York lay outside the car window—fast, electrifying contrasts, a huge open-air disco. Drink, dance, don't think. Braking and the regular rhythm of the engine. The lights of the signage overlapped and wove their colors, beating to a different drum in a symphony that not all could understand. They urged me to waste no more time.

The driver, a Latino, was observing us in the rear-view mirror. Seeing that no one was talking, he had upped the volume of the music. I knew the piece, *Libertango* by Astor Piazzolla. I liked it. It had a tinge of melancholy I felt was full of promise.

My thoughts had veered off again. From inside to out. I turned toward Anna and smiled at her. She looked frightened.

Yes, she was a child.

A woman-child, or the opposite.

It was a very hot night. Her hand was icy cold.

What was I doing?

Was there any need to guess?

Too much alcohol, that's what it was. Instinct had gotten the upper hand and had driven me out of the club together with her.

In the meantime, we had arrived. I paid the driver and we went into the lobby of my building.

"Try not to make any noise, please. Better not to wake my landlady." Anna nodded and slipped off her shoes. She had nice feet, small for her height. I opened the door and switched on the table lamp.

Only that one.

\*\*\*

Marco's apartment seemed different than the other times I had been there. It was an unknown place, alien.

"Would you like something to drink? Are you thirsty?" His tone was the kind you use with an important guest. Enchanted, I looked at him. He was bent slightly forward, illuminated by the fridge light. His skin was perfect.

I remembered my secret, my affliction, the reason why at nineteen I had stopped going to the beach. I was ashamed of what my clothes concealed.

Now I was there, alone with the man I had really fallen for, the first real love of my life.

Perhaps something was about to happen between him and me, finally. Perhaps the situation would go so far as to force me to reveal my scars? I had several on my hips and legs, but the thing that embarrassed me most and made me feel ugly, was the big scar that ran clean down my belly. A highway from beneath my bosom down to my pubes.

"Water," Marco said in the same tone as if he might say *champagne*! He came toward me holding a bottle of mineral water. I was leaning against the old wooden bureau. An ugly brown thing topped by a mirror.

Marco was looking at me and my reflection in the mirror. Before him he saw how I was, Anna with her bangs in disarray, her elbows resting on the top of the old bureau, the straps of her sandals with the slender heels still in the fingers of her left hand and her handbag clutched in the other. Behind me, in the mirror, I imagined my long dark hair, a cascade in the oval neckline that exposed my naked back. The curve of my shoulders betrayed all the tension of my insecurity.

"Do you want to stay or run for it?" He put the bottle down on the bureau and slipped his arms around my waist. "You don't know what to do, do you Anna?" He was serious.

I didn't reply. I was ready for anything. It was my moment, I felt it. Should I tell him that thing? No. Apart from the scars, he would notice it in any case. Would I look like a fool? Would he take it badly? Maybe he would reject me.

He kissed me, our first real kiss, closed up in a room. Alone. I looked him straight in the eye and knew I was on the first page of the book that would tell our story. But I wanted the fairy tale, with Marco, and I wanted to live it all the way.

"What is it?" He took my face between his hands and stared at me. My teeth began to chatter, quietly.

He noticed this and a little furrow appeared between his eyebrows. "What are we doing?" He detached himself from me. "Listen, it's too late for you to go home. Don't worry about a thing. I'll lend you some pajamas. Sleep here tonight." I stared at him wide eyed.

The atmosphere had changed, the moment, that moment, had slipped away without my noticing.

I was desperate. What was it that had gone wrong?

He didn't like me enough.

Maybe he had understood that...and he didn't like it.

Marco remained motionless, silent. I had no words.

I was ashamed. I couldn't understand a thing anymore.

Who was I? Why was everything going wrong?

Was it possible that I couldn't get over this thing?

I was ready. Ready!

Because I wanted him and no one else.

Finally he reacted. He smiled, but only with his mouth. "Come on, Anna. Don't be afraid. It doesn't matter. We'll sleep together and that's all. Like two good children."

And so it was. We slept in the same bed.

The first time.

Each on their own side of the mattress, in fact on the edge. After a while Marco began to snore gently.

That night I didn't sleep a wink. I wept and wept, in silence.

# 15
## THE NEXT DAY

"Fuck, Marco! Where did you get to yesterday evening?" Fabrizio looked as if he was making fun of me. It was early and there was no one in the office yet.

"I was tired. I wanted to get to bed before four in the morning. For once." I tossed that out there, but I knew that it wouldn't be enough for my friend. Sitting at my desk, I switched on the computer and pretended to concentrate on the documents in front of me.

That morning Anna had left very early to pass by her place to change before coming to the office. No way anyone could imagine she had spent the night in my room, in Pepita's house.

The girl had behaved responsibly.

No one was to see us arriving in the office together. No one was to suspect that there was something going on between us.

Anyway, nothing was going on. Nothing had happened.

Assuming that sharing the same bed for a whole night was nothing.

"Yesterday evening you disappeared with Anna. So, did the girl win?" Fabri said.

"Think what you want. Anna knows what she wants and in order to get it she's prepared to put herself out there," I replied curtly as I manipulated the mouse, my eyes glued to the screen.

"Are you saying she put out?"

"Hell, Fabrizio!"

"Good boys, at work already. Did you open the office?" Rosario Montrone made his theatrical entry. He wore a cordial expression, but there was no doubt that the time for goofing off was over.

It was time to get down to it. Fabrizio vanished into the office next door and I pretended to ignore Rosario's remark. He gave me a long questioning look. He said nothing, asked nothing. Thank god. Sometimes bosses have a particular sixth sense.

Of Anna, no trace. I hadn't recognized the sound of her footsteps along the corridor, nor the echo of her 'Good morning, good morning guys,' the greeting she spread around faithfully every morning, repeating it over and over as if she were handing out candy.

I caught myself thinking that I knew lots of things about her, but basically I knew nothing.

Anna was strong.

Once more I thought that Anna scared me.


A few days previously, Olympia had arrived; she was the intern who was to stand in for me for urgent matters when I was in Italy. More than anything else, she was there to give Rosario a hand. She was Swiss, from Lucerne, an unusual thing for our company, even though it employed people from all over the world. Unlike Anna's, Olympia's beauty was eye-catching, highlighted by the heavy makeup she wore even first thing in the morning, along with tight-fitting clothes and a vivacious manner, a bit over the top. She laughed a lot and invited laughter in return. In short, a Barbie.

I had to give her a few dossiers on business items that concerned Rosario and I found myself spending several hours in her company. Pleasant hours.

"How long have you been here?" Olympia interrupted me right in the middle of a complex explanation. The documents with the graphs were lying on the table in front of us.

We were alone and I decided we could take a break. I pushed my chair back and stretched out my legs as I clasped my hands behind the nape of my neck. "I got here in August two years ago, as soon as I heard about the internship. When I left Italy I was taking a big risk. I boarded the plane without even knowing where I was going to sleep." I glanced at her to see what effect my story was having. "I wasn't afraid of anything. I felt I was going to make it, that I could take on the world. Work didn't scare me, I was convinced that the future held goodness knows how many wonders in store for me and... I still think that, you know?"

"Like me," Olympia broke in. "My mother says I am a *forward girl*. She has a rather dated way of speaking." She came out with a long, modulated laugh that was so funny it was impossible to resist. "I told her, 'Mom, when I'm there I'll check out the situation and then I'll fend for myself,' but she always worries and hopes that I'll go back home when my internship is over."

"And will you go back?"

"Will you?"

"No, I don't think so. No one at home expects me to go back. Besides, things are going well for me here, they've hired me and prospects are good." I saw the scene of my first departure again. Matteo and Sofia standing in the kitchen, their backs against the sink, holding coffee cups in their hands. Seated at the table, my father kept on stirring the spoon in his cup. It was shortly before my flight from Ancona, less than three hours away. Sofia had looked at me, then she turned toward my brother. He drank his coffee and, putting the cup in the sink, he said, "You do realize, Sofia, that he won't come back anymore?"

In that moment I was thinking the same thing. I wouldn't be coming back; my life lay elsewhere.

"No regrets at having dropped everything and everybody?" Olympia had become serious.

"No, ours is an existence made of sacrifices. You spend most of your life in the office, you work a lot. Too much. But you're here, in the place where anything can happen. You get homesick, but you have important experiences, you meet people that you would never meet in Italy and you think about the sports field where you played soccer with your school friends, every Friday evening." My pals came to mind: Tommi, Mone, Farso, Richi, Baffo, Chicco, Filo. We grew up together and thought nothing would ever separate us. Now we had drifted apart from one another.

"I dreamed for years of coming here, to New York, and I still can't believe I'm here," she said.

"Here you make new friends, eat badly and dream about lasagna—the real stuff. But it's like going back to square one in your life. At least that's how it was for me. And you, what do you miss about Lucerne?" In the meantime, I had rolled my chair closer to hers.

I turned to get some papers and saw Anna in the doorway. There was no doubt she had been standing there for a few minutes, her face the picture of disappointment at finding me enjoying the company of another woman. She didn't stop, but went away immediately, without saying hello.

I felt a lump in my throat. I would have liked to go to her, but Olympia was there and the move wouldn't have escaped

144

her. There was no way I was going to let it get around that I was hooking up with an intern. Fabrizio knew, but I trusted him; then there was Zoe, who dropped hints, but had no certainties. At least as far as I was concerned. But what if Anna had told her something about us?

Was there an us? The question hung in the air. For the time being, I had other things to think about. I didn't want to attach too much importance to a strange evening born out of one drink too many. I thought about this, but in reality I couldn't wait to be alone with Anna again.

'Desire, more than the heart,' I told myself in a bid to convince myself that the situation was still under control. I was to realize later that it was already love.

The rest of the day went fast; Olympia was a diversion, even though in the middle of a laugh or an explanation of how to deal with the documents, a window would open before my eyes. I peered into Anna's soul, embittered because I had ignored her, maybe even a little jealous. I was sorry, but then I shrugged off the irritating guilty feelings and managed to smile again, thinking that in a few hours everything would change. I peeked inside the envelope containing my tickets and passport.

Then Anna again. Anna, Anna, Anna...Perhaps I had stopped myself just in time. Deep down I was pleased with my self-control; I wasn't going to make any wrong moves. My parachute was the departure for Italy. Within forty-eight hours I would be on the plane to go and be the best man at my brother and Sofia's wedding. There was no room for anything else.

Now that she was no longer in my presence, I could tell myself that Anna was just one girl among many. Who knows, a fling with her might have been fine, but I wasn't ever going to find out. I brushed Olympia's arm with my hand; she took a look around and came so close to me that I was enveloped in her scent, too powerful and sweet for me. Anna's instead... In any event, I had to find a way of saying goodbye to her before I left. It might be the last time we would meet. Yes, a goodbye was fitting, without any guile or ulterior motives, like good friends.

***

"Anna, wait." Marco caught up with me a few yards before the subway station. "We didn't see each other all day."

"I noticed you were very busy," I replied curtly.

He took me by the arm, something he had never done before, an unusual familiarity between us, not just friends anymore but not yet lovers. We were in a dough made of flour, milk, eggs and honey that was rising with one breath after another. So very softly, like a puff of air.

"I need to set things right." Marco wore a smirk and I figured he was pleased about my jealousy. I tried to take my arm from his, but he grabbed my hand, "Forgive me, even though I have done nothing to be forgiven for. Believe me." He left the request hanging in the air, then gave me a sidelong look. His expression changed and he grew serious: "Let's go to my place. I have some frozen pizza in the fridge."

"Ooh, luxury!" I exclaimed ironically, but I wasn't sore anymore. His invitation had completely changed my mood yet again and once more I felt the whirl of feelings I had for Marco begin to churn once more. A shake made with many different ingredients that was about to overflow.

Now I would have willingly cooked for him. Never mind frozen pizza.

During the subway ride we didn't speak much, but touched each other with our eyes, fleeting glances, that were occasionally more intense and then broken off. I looked at him again as he stared at the cuff of his jacket sleeve. It seemed as if his eyes were attached to all that gray, but with an involuntary dart they came back to me for a second. I felt warm and to change the atmosphere, I observed the backpack of the homeless guy slumped on the seat facing me. My eyes like an airport metal detector, I X-rayed the few things he had with him until, without wanting to, I got lost again in Marco's chin, on the fuzz of his one-day beard, and then moved up to his nose and the shape of his eyes. Halfway home I found a seat. I was in front of him and his legs were pressed against my knees. There was a tension, the kind you feel when you know that what will happen in the next few hours will determine the course of your life.

A bet.

\*\*\*

We went into the house without making a sound. No one noticed our arrival: not Pepita and not even Simone who was perhaps already in his room. As for Fabrizio, I knew he had stayed on at the office to finish a job that would keep him busy for a good while.

We didn't open the fridge, nor did we turn on the oven. We embraced as soon as I closed the door of my apartment behind us.

Anna didn't speak. She stared at me, eyes moist and slightly blurred like the evening we had slept together. She was concealing something from me, I felt it. We ended up lying on the bed in an embrace made of kisses. Instinctively, I realized

I had to go slowly even though she now seemed more at ease. She smiled as she caressed me awkwardly. Yes, there was some embarrassment.

I liked it that she, so bold in courting me, was shy now. Even too much so—it confused me. I tried to understand her uneasiness, tried to decode the signals her body was sending me—she was expressing apprehension, but also desire.

"Do you want to?" I asked her in a low voice, caressing her under her chin.

"Yes, but there's something I have to tell you," she said in one breath.

"You don't have to tell me anything, Anna. Let yourself go."

I unzipped her dress as she fumbled with the buttons of my shirt. She took refuge under the sheet. It was hot, but I followed her.

"Marco." She buried her face in the hollow of my neck and came close.

Anna let herself be guided.

She simply didn't know how and wasn't good at improvising. At least not yet. It had been ages since I had found myself in a similar situation. Years.

For a moment I thought of backing out, then I immediately forgot that idea. I was overwhelmed by her way of making love, awkward and sweet, welcoming and gauche. Even a little childish. That was the occasion on which we slipped together into our love story as if it were the most natural thing in the world.

I realized I was no longer afraid of Anna. Now she was mine.

The next morning I took her coffee in bed. It was six in the morning; we hadn't slept much and she struggled to wake up.

She seemed amazed to see me, then she opened up in a smile that was almost burning; like the sunshine already filtering through the windows, it was too hot. I held out the cup and immediately drew back.

"Why are you afraid of me?" She asked with a pout.

She wasn't as easy and predictable as she seemed. Anna, so delicate, was made of steel.

"Sure I am." I kissed her. "I'm leaving today, did you forget? I've still got lots to do, things I had planned to sort out yesterday evening. But, as you know, the evening changed course." I laughed, took the empty cup from her hands and put it on the bedside table. I stretched out on the bed, fully clothed, and kissed her. "I have to go to the office," I said in a low voice. Anna sighed and drew the sheet up to her chin.

"Take your time. Just try not to be seen when you leave," I told her.

"I know. I'll be careful. In the office I'll treat you badly." She threw the pillow at me, laughing. "Stay away from Olympia, otherwise..." Her expression was beatific.

"I won't be there." I saw her face darken and I liked that. I was in a real poor state. "But now I have to go. Would you believe I left my tickets and passport on my desk?"

"You didn't!"

"Your fault. Yesterday evening I was in a rush, running after you."

I went out into the dewy New York morning. The street was still fairly quiet, but already several people were heading for the subway station.

*  *  *

As soon as I was alone I burst into a flood of tears. I was happy and afraid.

149

I had made love for the first time with the man I had fallen for. I couldn't wait to be with Marco again, and instead he was leaving.

I was no longer a virgin.

My mother would have said I had become a woman.

Officially.

I needed to tell someone. Certainly not my mother. I didn't even stop to think about the time difference with Italy. In the room, the sun illuminated the part of the wall with the pillar clad in red brick. The light created a palette of shades on the blue sheet, and an unbearable pall of heat descended on the room. Marco had warned me—the air conditioning worked in fits and starts. It had been out of order the evening before, when it breathed out the last puff of cool air.

"Bea."

"Anna, I was just about to eat."

"You know Marco, the guy I've fallen in love with...well, I've been with him."

"So! Okay, so what? You're calling me to tell me that? Great news. Good for you, for both of you. If it was any good, that is." She sniggered.

"You don't get it. We made love." I paused for a moment. "For me it was the first time. I'm going to marry him," I added.

"You were still a virgin?" Bea was angry. I heard her moving. I imagined her walking along the corridor in her house, a long dark tunnel. "You never told me that. Why?"

"Well...You and the others were more expert than me. I never said anything one way or the other. Neither did I ever say I had done it with someone."

"You bitch. So you never went all the way with anyone. Besides..."

150

"It's nothing to be ashamed of. What's more, it's a problem solved, I guess." I laughed at my having found virginity an encumbrance. Finally I was free of that and with the right man. My man.

"It was high time it happened to you. End of story," she said, to get rid of me.

"End of nothing." Bea was unbearable and I was spending a fortune on that dumb call. "It was fantastic. It's the real thing with Marco. He's the man of my life."

"What an idiot you are. You're nothing but a kid and you're living in a fantasy world all by yourself. As usual," Bea replied, and continued: "I've already told you that, I believe. Listen to me..."

I ended the conversation without saying goodbye, but the bitter taste Bea had left me with didn't last long. Lying on the bed, I thought about Marco once more, about what had happened, about how I must have struck him as clumsy right from the foreplay and his expression when he realized...I hugged his pillow and thought about the next time. Oh god, would there be a next time? Yes, I was sure that that night marked a beginning. And besides, he had loved my scars, he had run his fingers over them backward and forward, a gentle, repeated caress. Then he had taken my hand to lead it to the mark left by the cut through which, when he was a boy, they had removed a kidney.

I had lost the sense of time and all that daydreaming made me late for work. I was stunned, happy and sad because within a few hours Marco would be leaving.

"Aren't you well, Anna?" Rosario surprised me as I was tottering toward my workstation.

"Thanks, everything's okay." I blushed. "I suffer from low blood pressure. The difference between the heat outside and the chill in here..."

"Drink some coffee, it'll do you good." He gave me an inquisitorial look. "In fact, take the day off."

He laid a hand on my shoulder to make me stop, then he took a long look at me. "You look like a ghost. I'll let Jeff know, and human resources, too," he said reassuringly.

I thought it was a miracle, a favorable alignment of the stars of the kind that happen only once in life. I would be able to see Marco before he left. I took a cab and went back to Pepita's house. He was there, busy finishing packing. He wasn't expecting me.

Now the tension between us was terrific. There wasn't time to do anything except talk and we wasted it telling each other pointless things: 'Have you taken this and that, and don't forget that other thing.' Every word meant something different than its formal sense; a demure way to express emotions and feelings by talking about toothbrushes or boarding passes. We brushed against each other and sparks flew.

"Anna." Marco looked at me, laying his hands on my shoulders. Once more I felt shy in his presence. I expected and at the same time feared his words. The door opened.

"Well, are you off? Did you think I wouldn't come to say goodbye?" Fabrizio came in, causing confusion. We hadn't even heard him knock.

"I called the cab. We agreed I would take you to the airport, remember?" Are you coming too, Anna? By the way, how come you're here?" His voice died away, hesitant. Perhaps he had got the message or at least suspected that something had happened between us.

Marco gave my hands a strong squeeze, then let them go and kissed me on the cheek. "Don't come," he whispered. "There'll be time. Just for us," and he added, "I've told Pepita that you'll be moving in here, today. It's all arranged."

"Ciao, Marco. Have a good trip," I said with as much non-chalance as I could muster. I closed my eyes and didn't open them again until I heard the door closing.

The room was empty.

Marco had gone.

# 16
## ANNA, WAIT!

I spent the hours in the plane that was taking me to Italy sunk in a drowse from which I emerged every so often to daydream. Everything that had happened in the last few days, my inevitable surrender to Anna...On what impulse? Sure, I had given in to my desire for her, after all, Anna had been provoking me for weeks, but I was well aware that behind what happened there was much more. The discovery that it was the first time she had made love, as if she had been waiting for me all her life, her candor, her unwitting, sexy innocence, her determination. Now my personal outlook for the future had completely changed, because of a woman. What had happened was the very thing I had intended to avoid.

When you come to a crossroads you don't know, you stop to think things over—that's normal. Taking the road you think is the right one will lead to a series of ineluctable consequences, for better or for worse, then there is the imponderable, the thing you would never expect but can happen anyway, an event beyond your control that you must adapt to.

I was well aware that life is never predictable. You have to accept a fate you can't always elude. Yet I was shaken in a way I hadn't been for years, perhaps since my mother died. Who was I? What did I really want from life? And again, why did life have to be so demanding, a constant obligation to try to tell what was working fine from what wasn't going to work at all? I would have preferred to carry on living without giving myself too much to do and, as a matter of fact, in New York I lived inside the niche I had built for myself: work, a few casual affairs, and then more work. I had always thought that for some time, yet I wouldn't have other needs to satisfy. My routine seemed perfect to me.

Now that time was over. I was at the famous crossroads and I hadn't even understood what kind of person I was.

Because of a girl.


The journey seemed longer and more tiring than usual and I arrived in Fano dog-tired. My father and brother realized that and let me rest, putting off until the next day what there was to say. I needed to get over the jet lag and I was snoozing on the couch in the living room when the sound of light footsteps brought me back to the surface. Sofia, Matteo's bride-to-be, had come into the room. I lay motionless, looking at her though half closed eyes. She was wonderfully beautiful.

"Hey, Marco, something on your mind? I'm the one who should be worried." She had realized I was awake. "A penny for your thoughts?" She winked.

I sat up, still sunk in the old worn-out cushions. That room had too much brown for us, so young and colorful. I noticed the contrast because Sofia radiated light all around her as she counted in an undertone the little white tulle bags of sugared almonds. Five per bag.

"Nothing. I wasn't thinking of anything. The usual things," I replied.

"This time you're not telling me the whole story." She peered into my soul with her eyes. "You're not talking. So something serious is going on. Who is it? How is it?"

"A beautiful girl; a piece of work just like you. No, I'm kidding, Sofi. Nothing serious. You know how it is. You work a lot, you have a night out and you keep the wheels of the economy turning." I gave a smart-alecky laugh.

"I won't insist, I have to go now. I'm getting married tomorrow, you know." She began to put the little bags in a wide, low box. Her eyes were sparkling. "It'll be your turn next. I get the feeling that someone's going to lead you to the altar."

I spread out my arms and shrugged, "The woman who manages to trap me hasn't been born yet."

"I don't know why, but I'm convinced something good is going to happen to you. I get the feeling that there's someone who's either in your life or is about to come..."

"Are you kidding, Sofia?"

She planted herself in front of me, took my hands and squeezed them firmly. "Do you know that when you left I felt bad? I was happy for you, but I lost my friend, my ally in this family. My rock, in other words."

"That's not true, I was always there for you."

"Yes, I found that out later, but I didn't know it then."

Sofia broke into a broad smile and tilted her head a little to one side.

Anna's face was superimposed on hers. I wished she had been with me. For a moment I thought of her as my house. In the meantime, my future sister-in-law was talking again. "You were present on the day I graduated and you were happy to be there; that made you extraordinary in my eyes. You were always there even after that, from a distance. Remember when things between Matteo and me were on the verge of going wrong? You helped us. I still have the mail we wrote to each other."

I noticed that her eyes were shining and at that point I was moved, too. "That'll do, Sofia...You're risking becoming the bride with dark circles under her eyes. I have to stay on top of things, too; the best man must be in top form. But why I let myself be persuaded to be your chauffeur, too, I really don't know." We hugged, then she said, "We have some great memories, but the best is yet to come. For all of us."

The best.

Anna would be my best. In that moment it was clear to me. It had taken me a while to realize that, but now I was sure. I didn't have to fear Anna, I just had to love her. I couldn't wait to hold her again, to talk to her. I imagined our meeting, her questioning look, her smile after she had heard what I had to say to her. The echo of her laugh came to me, sincere, sparkling. And then we would have an endless time in which to savor life.

The next day in church, as the priest celebrated Matteo and Sofia's wedding, I was dreaming about Anna and me sitting on a red couch, leafing through our album of memories. We reviewed all our conquests, the things we had succeeded in doing, and talked about our future projects.

It was evening, we had eaten and I was sure that a child was sleeping in the other room.

Our child.

Anna's child and mine.

\*\*\*

After he left for Italy he didn't get in touch for two days. Forty-eight hours in which I changed into a phantom roaming the streets of New York. I went down into the subway and came up onto the street, always with my head lowered, my hair like a window shade because everything going on around me was pointless, it didn't interest me. Every minute of the ride between Pepita's house, into which I had moved, to the office and back was devoted to making an orderly list of the reasons why he hadn't called.

Marco had lent me his apartment, but being there among his things and feeling his absence, not because he was far away, but because he was ignoring me, was unbearable. On the third day he called me. It was early morning and I was already awake after a disturbed night in which I had slept only intermittently and never for long.

"The ceremony starts in an hour," he said. "I don't have much time and I have several things to do."

"So go. Do what you have to do." My tone was chilly. I was sitting in the center of the bed, my shoulders bowed, my unkempt hair covering my face and big tears flowing down my cheeks and running down the neck of my tank top. I was prepared for the worst, but also determined to hang in there. There was no way Marco was going to hear my voice shake.

"First I have to tell you something important. I care about you, Anna. Yes, we are in a relationship." Overwhelmed, I said nothing. "Are you there? Did you hear me?"

"Yes."

"We are together. Will you wait for me?"

"Yes."

"You're sure not very demonstrative!" Some background noises—voices—came to me. Someone was calling him. "I have to go. Bye, Princess," Marco said.

"I'm waiting for you, love," I replied and stopped there. The ice inside me had melted. A fever of happiness welled up in me that made me sweat. I was still sitting on the bed, but now my shoulders were straight, my back propped up by my arms planted in the mattress, my head tilted back and my hair hanging down to the sheets. The graying ceiling crisscrossed with a few cobwebs was a dazzling supernova to my eyes.

From then on everything changed. I changed, too. Marco returned a few days afterward and then it was my turn to leave for Italy. My internship with Valentino was over. I was determined to find another job opportunity that would take me back to New York, for now Marco was my home. He was my love, my friend and confidant, my mentor, and my playmate. I had to understand, we had to understand together, how solid our relationship was, something on which to build the rest of our lives.


I arrived in Venice on Sunday morning. My parents were at the airport with Raffi, my brother. We were happy to see one another; after all, for the past three months our contact had been limited to phone calls.

"You look beautiful, Anna." My mother hugged me to her and then pushed me back a little to check me out, her arms outstretched and her hand gripping my elbow almost as if she feared that I might fly away like a helium balloon.

"You look beautiful, too," I replied. "You are all beautiful." I enfolded them in a collective hug. I wanted to shift attention away from me. I was tired after the flight, and I wasn't ready to talk about Marco.

"You look really good, you know?" Now dad was getting involved. Anyway, I was feeling beautiful. When you're in love, it shines through from every pore.

"Did you bring presents?" I thanked heaven for having a brother, and all the way home they sat spellbound as I told them about the wonders of my stay in New York.

160

Between one round of conversation and the next I didn't notice we had arrived. The car entered the driveway. The leaves on the trees were already streaked with yellow, and the green of the grass was less vivid. As soon as I went inside I found the aroma of coffee, and the smell of laundry and tobacco that I remembered.

"Do you mind if I lie down for a while? Only an hour or so."

"Go, child," Mom said. "I'll wake you for lunch. I've made rice salad, veal with tuna sauce, salad with peanuts..."

"Ah, that one!"

"Why?"

"Nothing. I'm glad. I had a real hankering for that."

To go to my room I passed by the dining room. My mother had already set a festive table in my honor. The tablecloth was Flanders linen.

"See you later," I said with a loud yawn.

"My beautiful little girl," she murmured sweetly. Dad and Raffi had disappeared somewhere or other. Maybe messing about in the garage, as usual.

In my room everything was as I had left it. But I was very different than the gauche little girl who had left three months before. I slipped off my sandals and dropped onto the single bed. It seemed small. One minute later, I was asleep.

Lunch with the whole family and a few friends, about twenty people in all, was tiring. I was the center of attention and I could hardly eat as I replied to the questions that came from all around the table. In the afternoon I finished handing out the presents and Bea dropped by, too. We went to my room where I had some other packages. Bea was strangely nice; she fawned on me at length. "So, how's it going with that hunk you made it with?" The question came out straight after she had beaten around the bush for a half hour, without success.

I replied with a laugh as I got to my feet to pick up the crumpled gift paper.

"Well, aren't you going to give me some details?" Bea was insistent, her tone honeyed. I felt my irritation grow. Did she take me for an idiot? What did she want, she who had never gone farther than Venice?

"I'm hungry. I feel like some Nutella." I opened the door and went out into the hallway, then ran down the stairs.

I heard Bea get up and follow me, panting.

"Wait! You've only just got here and you're not giving me any news." She had been my best friend, the one who explained the ways of the world to me and for years I had held her opinion in high regard, but she was just a bitch. I waited for her down in the lobby, the door open for her to leave.

"Ciao, Bea," I said. "Thanks for coming. Goodbye." She didn't respond to my last farewell.

Mom. I needed to talk to Mom. I had to find the right occasion. It came the next morning. As soon as I finished breakfast I knew it was my moment. Besides, the two of us were alone in the house. No one would disturb us for a few hours.

"What would you like to eat today, treasure?"

"Whatever you feel like cooking."

"Now that you're here you can put on a few pounds. You're so thin. Over there you didn't eat properly and you can see that. A good thing you came back home." Mom was talking in front of the open fridge door. She fished some zucchini out of the vegetable bin.

"Yes, I've come back, but I intend to leave again." I was sitting at the kitchen table, smoothing the cotton tablecloth with slow movements of my hand. In front of me there was my empty coffee cup and the jar of marmalade I had just opened.

"If you're through, close the marmalade." She slammed the fridge door and turned around, then she dropped into the chair in front of me. "What do you mean?" Her tone had gone up one octave.

"My dissertation is almost finished. In the meantime I'm going to look for another internship over there. There's a guy who's waiting for me. We live together." That *we live together* contained the revelation of an intimate detail, a confession from woman to woman. My mother lowered her gaze to her apron, sighed and clasped her hands in her lap, without saying anything.

I let her absorb the news. The sound of the clock filled the room, then from outside came the muffled braying of a donkey and a rumble of thunder.

"Is he American?"

"He's Italian."

She straightened up, her look intelligent and lively once more. Mom can take a hit. "Tell me he's from the Veneto. A man from here, one of us."

"No." I burst out laughing. "He's an outsider. From the Marche, imagine that..."

"From the sea? Does he live on the coast?"

"Yes, in Fano. It would have been the same if he had lived in the mountains or in an inland city. What's that got to do with anything?"

Silence. It was obvious she was measuring her words. She reached across the table and took my hands. "Tell me about him. His family?"

"Normal. Good people. His father is retired. He has an older brother, just married."

"I want to know about his mom. What's she like? Have you spoken to her? Did you meet her and then, what's his name, what does he do? So, where did this fellow pop up from?" She let my hands go and leaned against the chair back. Ready to listen.

"Marco," I smiled. "Marco Falcioni, handsome as can be. He's been in New York for two years, hired by Valentino, a good job with great career prospects." I wanted to score a point straight off to overcome her resistance. The work situation of any future son-in-law was a sensitive issue for all mothers. Mine was no exception, in fact, I noticed she had relaxed.

"There's plenty like that around here, too. But you always have to be different." She glanced out the window. The light in the kitchen had changed, and the sky was a blue black, heralding a late summer storm. Mom concentrated on me once more. Her gaze was calm and benign.

I figured I had almost got over the obstacle. Almost. "He has no mother. Sadly, she died when he was fifteen. She was hit by a truck. She was riding her bicycle, just like folks do around here. Marco was very close to her..."

"Poor thing!" she broke in. Now she looked bewildered. "It's not good to grow up without a mother. What did his father do?"

"Nothing. He didn't remarry if that's what you want to know. The three of them made a family, three men alone. They got by." She shook her head and I decided to spill the beans. "Marco knows how to get over difficulties. He learned when he was small. When he was eighteen months old he had a tumor. They removed a kidney and he got better. His mother did whatever it took, his brother too. Marco told me..."

"He's sick. Forget him."

"Mom. What are you saying? He's perfectly well."

"You never can tell. Forget him. You must stay with us now. You've been over there, you tried, you saw. Enough!

We're not a family of migrants. You'll stay here and you'll settle down. You'll find someone, like everybody else." I wasn't expecting this kind of talk and I didn't recognize my mother. My folks weren't freethinkers, but this narrow-mindedness...A mixture of irritation and impatience began to grow inside me.

"Mom, don't talk nonsense."

"Show your mother respect."

"And you do the same to me. I'm not a child anymore and I know what I must do."

"No, you don't." Now she got to her feet and took off her apron. "You'll see what your father will say. Did you tell Bea?"

"You're the first and only one to know." My voice was shaking. The disappointment! "I was sure you would be happy for me and all you do is talk nonsense."

"Again! Show some respect, child," she yelled. "And you want to take on a man who's half sick...You fool! What if you find yourself alone at thirty? Have you thought of that?"

I wouldn't have ever believed it possible to hear my mother say anything like that.

I jumped to my feet and went out of the kitchen. I grabbed my bag from the peg in the hallway and ran out, letting the front door slam behind me. The wind was raising flurries of dirt and leaves as the first fat raindrops began to fall; lightning lit up the morning that had suddenly become dark as night. A commotion similar to that of the sky above churned within me; my certainties—the confidence that my mother would have welcomed my love for Marco—everything had been swept away. I was disappointed, lost, alone and so angry I couldn't even cry. I would never forget the words my mother had struck me with, even though I know she didn't entirely mean what she had said. It was a way to keep me within her borders, those of the family, which was no longer mine. My frontier, my land and my home all lay with Marco.

I didn't give up. Doggedly, I went ahead. I had chosen another life: with Marco I would go all the way. My country's way of thinking, the imaginary limits connected to my being a woman, the shackles of tradition, were all garbage I felt had nothing to do with me. I was no longer the Anna who had left for New York a few months before. The change had been rapid; I had done away with the useless baggage I had taken with me at first. Now I was traveling light and at peace with myself.

Relations with my folks were tense for some time. Every so often they granted me a respite and the atmosphere at home was more relaxed. Perhaps they hoped that over time I might forget Marco, but he and I were planning our future together while I looked for a job that would allow me to stay in New York. In the family, when the talk got around to my graduation, I always repeated that I would be leaving after that and the ill feeling would start over.

Graduation day came. I already had my ticket to return to New York, to Marco. A new job was waiting for me there, in finance.

# 17
## RETURN TO NEW YORK

*November 2006*

"What are you up to? Spring cleaning?" Fabrizio had stretched out on my bed as I cleaned the fridge.

"Marco, I'm talking to you. Aren't we going out this evening?"

"Can't you see I'm busy?" I had collected stacks of jars of sauces and pickles. Many were past their expiration date and needed to be thrown out.

"It's not like Anna's coming tomorrow. But I'm leaving in three days. Did you forget?"

"No, but I want her to find everything clean and tidy."

"That doesn't authorize you to be a jerk with me, for fuck's sake." He sat up on the bed, giving me a black look. He had made his decision: he was going back to Italy for keeps and god knows when I would see him again.

"Come on, Fabri. Have a little patience, then we'll go. I envy you. I'd like to go back home, too." I lied to console him for what he was leaving and sooner or later would maybe regret.

"Liar. You couldn't give a damn. All you think of is Anna. I can already see you two married with kids. Old together. We'll meet up on vacation in Fano, on the benches along the seafront."

"Yes, we'll have sticks and false teeth." The fridge was okay. I closed the bag of garbage.

"Our wives will have false teeth, too."

"Not Anna. She'll always be the way she is now. Come on, let's go have some fun."

"What a dick. Well, shall we go chase some tail?" He was kidding, and I pretended to slap him on the head. I was very fond of him. Anna and I would miss him; the trio would be disbanded before she arrived.

She came back on a rainy day. New York was steaming under a muggy pall that made even your thoughts foggy. When I kissed her, the umbrella tilted backward and we got soaked. That was a good thing because she didn't notice that the drops running down my face were tears of gratitude. Not that I would ever have admitted that to her.

I had fixed up Pepita's old apartment as best I could. Seeing Anna's baggage scattered around, watching her as she put her clothes in the closet, moved me. She arrived on a Friday and we spent the weekend making love. And eating. Anna fixed my favorite dishes and some others I didn't recognize, recipes from her part of Italy. Our first Sunday evening together, I wanted to surprise her by making one of the few recipes I could do well: veal scaloppini in lemon sauce. I served it up. She sniffed the aroma, took her knife and fork and carefully cut the meat, dipped it into the sauce and tasted it. She gaped in amazement and lavished compliments on what a great chef I was. Ever after, the crafty thing would bring up my skills with veal scaloppini every time she didn't feel like cooking.

Sharing the house struck us as natural. She moved gracefully among the ugly furniture. She laughed gracefully, she made love gracefully. Yes, I was crazy about her. I thought about my resistance of a few months before and couldn't understand it. We were destined to be together.

In the evening, when we met up after work, everything was new. An encounter that was as exciting as if it had been the first meeting of two lovers. She would often come to meet me after work and wait for me in the street outside the building. "Hi, sweetheart. May I give you a hug?" She would kiss me furtively. "Let's get out of here. We mustn't let anyone see us." She pretended to have to respect the rule of when we both worked together at Valentino, where love between colleagues was not advisable. She played, she acted, she made me little surprises. We often went out with friends, but we liked being alone, too.

Working in a milieu like finance, an almost exclusively male preserve, wasn't easy for her, but Anna seemed to have found an equilibrium. Every so often, however, there was a price to pay.

One evening we decided to eat out just the two of us. I had noticed her ill humor and that's why I took her to one of our favorite places, Max SoHa, a stone's throw from Columbia University and our place. It was cheap and the food was good. Anna had opened her mouth only to order a salad with fennel and arugula, to be eaten after an appetizer of prosciutto and mozzarella, while I opted for macaroni Sicilian style.

"What a bunch of rats," she burst out after having played around with her salad for a while. She still hadn't eaten anything, limiting herself to a glass of wine that had loosened her tongue.

"What happened? I haven't asked you anything until now, but I know there's something wrong. Come on, Anna, talk to me."

"Until today I thought I was like the others, one of them. I made an effort. Look at me, even now I'm wearing their uniform and god knows what a drag it is to wear these repugnant black suits." She was talking fast and mumbling.

"Calm down. Have a drop of wine. Eat something and then go on. We're in no hurry." I'd never seen her so steamed up.

She took a sip of wine. "This afternoon I was talking over the phone with a client. I was explaining our offer to him and I was doing it in the right kind of professional tone. He was pressing me, so I went through it point by point so that everything was clear. The guy was agitated, in a rush." She left that hanging in the air for a few seconds and then said in a voice that was rather too loud. "A rush for what, besides?" I looked around a bit uneasily, but no one seemed to be paying any attention to us. Then she said, "At a certain point he interrupted me, saying, 'Speak English, speak English!' I kept calm and started over and he got nasty, saying hysterically: 'I don't want to speak with some damned immigrant.' Can you believe that?" I noticed her chin was trembling.

"Anna, you were dealing with a moron. Forget it." I tried to console her, but she was furious. I couldn't bear her having to suffer such humiliation.

"My accent. You can still hear I'm a foreigner. I must lose the accent. People on the other end of the phone don't want to deal with a woman and especially not one with a foreign accent. They don't trust you."

"Anna, for every one like that there are a hundred who don't care about your accent and have confidence in you."

"No. You're a man, you don't understand. Anyway, I'm going to lose my accent. That's the least I can do. But I've had it. I can't take it anymore." After the outburst she began to eat.

170

We even managed to end the dinner with a few laughs—the worst was over. She wanted to pay the check and left an excessive tip for the Mexican waitress.

Our bond grew with every passing day. In the hours when we were apart we both longed for each other. Friends looked on us with affection, sympathy, irony, and some even with a tinge of envy.

"We're going home for Christmas. You to my house and I to yours." We were in the subway at rush hour, crammed in among the Friday evening crowd. My tone suggested a decision already made. Anna seemed surprised at first, then she returned my smile.

So, that December of 2006 we made our first stopover in my town by the sea. My father and brother loved her straight off. Sofia, too. I had the feeling they were destined to become friends.

Early one morning I caught Anna standing in the dining room looking at the photo of my mother, an enlargement of the one I always carried with me.

"What do you think of her?" I asked.

"She looks so wistful. Your heart goes out to her. A beautiful woman. The bouffant hairdo, the oval face and the dress cinched tight around the waist, that lovely flared skirt. The fashion in those days." Then she pointed to another photo in which my mother was standing in a stiff, rather odd pose. "It looks like certain photos of my mom from that same period." She said nothing for a while. "Who knows what torment she went through when you got sick."

Anna became sad, but only for a moment. She turned around to kiss me. "Here everything has stood still, just like in my house. I bet these ornaments are the same ones Cristina chose. You haven't even moved them around. Can you smell the odors of mustiness mixed with freshness and apples? I recognize the silence, too, a silence I had forgotten."

"We're not used to it anymore. There isn't a silence like this at any time of day or night in our place." New York pulsated unceasingly. Quiet didn't exist. As for the smells, those were altogether different.

"I like your family, but I couldn't live here. Not even in my home, with my parents." She sighed and pirouetted with arms widespread, her hair following the movement of her body like a banner. I grabbed her hands and forced her to sink into the old brown couch together with me.

"Here they've been left behind. At most they're interested in preserving what they have. And that's another reason why we left." I hugged her. "We're going ahead. Each time we come back here we'll discover that nothing has changed. After all, it's convenient for us to find our old things as we remember them."

"I don't know," she said. "Wait till you meet Sveva, my mother." I knew that Anna feared this meeting. She hadn't concealed how much her folks were against our relationship.

I couldn't foresee what might happen either.

"Your mother will adore me. All the mothers of my fiancées adore me." I was kidding in order to take the edge off her anxiety. "In any case, afterward we'll go to the mountains. We can relax."

"At least we can forget the hassles, if things should go badly." She kissed me behind my ear.

"On the contrary. I'm sure it'll go fine." Anna, so strong and determined, was afraid of tensions in the family. All in all, I understood her. I had often been a buffer between my father and my brother. Our family had suffered from the absence of a woman: our feelings were unrefined, and never shown. Our

172

relations were barren even of words, then Sofia had come along and much had changed. Even my father had mellowed, in his own way.

The countryside of the Veneto unfolded outside the window. Anna hadn't opened her mouth in the last half hour. I commented on the landscape and she replied in monosyllables. The gate of her house was already open, a sign that we were expected. As we got out of the car, a woman appeared in the doorway of the house.

"Welcome," she said, in a clipped tone. I headed toward her wearing my best smile.

"Mom, this is Marco. Marco, Sveva."

Sveva kissed us and gave Anna a lengthy hug. "Come on in. Coffee's ready. Are you hungry?"

"Thank you, ma'am. I never say no to a coffee. As for hunger..."

"Oh, it's only apple pie. I always make it." I realized she wanted to keep me at a distance.

"Well if Anna learned to cook from you, I'll willingly take pie. Your daughter spoils me. She's a great cook." Anna said nothing as she hung her jacket and bag on the coat stand by the front door. I immediately followed Sveva into the kitchen.

"You live in a magnificent spot," I said. "A lovely house. Do you look after the garden?"

"My husband and I both do some. He'll be here soon. Take a seat. You too, Anna." More than an invitation, it was an order. I was under scrutiny. We planned to stay there for a week, like at my house. I decided I had to play my cards straight off, otherwise our stay would be only a source of tensions. "Anna, you didn't tell me your mother was so young. I always have trouble imagining the age of mothers." As I was speaking I was turned toward Sveva. "Or I imagine them as very young, with a baby in their arms or later on, surrounded by grandchildren."

"Have some pie." Sveva set down a tray with three cups of coffee and two plates holding two huge slices. "I know you have no mother," she added in sweeter tones. I didn't reply, I just took the coffee and started to blow softly on the scalding black liquid. I didn't do that in a calculated way; there, between the mother and daughter, who she was trying to defend from a threat that was in reality imaginary, a lump came into my throat. I would have wanted a mother like that. In fact, I wished my mother was with us. I would have liked to see her chatting with Anna's mother. Two women worried about our future. Maybe it was that silence, drawn out for too long, because even one minute can be endless on certain occasions, or maybe Sveva sensed my uneasiness, but from then on she began to soften. Anna noticed this, too.

Sveva took us upstairs. Anna hesitated for a moment when she got to the top of the stairs.

"You know the way." Sveva said. "Marco, you'll be sleeping in Anna's brother Raffi's room. He'll be coming later, too. We sleep there," she added. Anna's parents' room served as a divide between ours. "Is that all right?" she said.

"Perfect, ma'am, thanks." In the meantime, I opened the bedroom door. Outside the window there was a vineyard shrouded in mist. "That's lovely! I always say to Anna that man can't live by concrete alone." Sveva smiled, but she wasn't yet through sizing me up.

"Get your bags inside and settle in. Anna, will you give me a hand in the kitchen?"

"Coming."

"Show him around. The bathroom. See if he needs anything. I've done all I can, but you Americans have different habits."

"Not at all, ma'am. I'm Italian, native of the Marche and adoptive Venetian on the girlfriend's side. Finally she gave me a real smile. "Enough of this *ma'am*. Call me Sveva." Behind her, Anna's face lit up.

# 18
# MY MOTHER'S DARLING

Marco had become my mother's darling, her third child. They had both won each other over within a few hours. Another love at first sight to which Marco had shamelessly surrendered. I was happy because I loved both of them and also because the way things had gone meant we would have an easy time of it regarding a whole bunch of issues, but every so often it weighed on me.

"Give me a hand, Anna. I still have to make the pasta for the lasagna. You keep an eye on the sauce."

"Not lasagna again," I said.

"Marco likes it, the poor boy."

"Why poor boy? I can't stand lasagna anymore. Even dad and Raffi are sick of it."

"I decide what we eat. That'll do."

Marco appeared in the kitchen doorway, the usual dazzling smile on his lips; he was cocooned in a red Ferrari sweatshirt, a Christmas gift from his brother.

"My favorite ladies of the stove, good morning."

"You're not going to charm *me*," I said.

"Anna, my love, be nice."

"Do as Marco says," my mother said. "She certainly can't make you lasagna like mine." She addressed Marco again.

"Television has definitely influenced her about many things. You know Antonella Clerici, the presenter who does that cookery show? Anna thinks she's a goddess come to Earth, or rather to the kitchen."

"What's that got to do with anything? I didn't only watch that." Marco was looking me in amusement.

"Of course not. After the accident you were glued to that Licia Colò, the woman who did the travel program, the one about Kilimanjaro."

"Oh yes?" Marco had put on a sly expression. I shot him a withering glance, but he decided to press on. "And what else did she learn from television?"

"She got her mania for travel from Colò, that's for sure." My mother was unstoppable.

"So what?" I tried to say my piece. "It's not like I was glued to the screen all day long. In any case, I couldn't walk, remember? I started surfing the net."

"Yes, she got Internet mania." Heaven knows why, but Sveva had fixed sandwiches for Marco. She pushed the plate toward him with a smile. Marco smiled back and nodded in a token of satisfaction, then took a bite. By now the understanding between them was perfect, and they had no need to speak.

"I did a bunch of things online: art, history, even interior design. I learned all about the Cuban revolution, Perestroika and the war in Vietnam. All stuff they don't teach you at school. I even became a lover of the Impressionists; you know Monet and Giverny? One day we'll go there and we'll go to Normandy too, to see the light and the colors that inspired them. Maybe on our honeymoon..." I was joking, I wanted to break the circle between those two and I succeeded. For a moment they dropped the air of condescension they

178

bore toward me, which had been irritating me a little. I had succeeded and as I had their complete attention, I decided to leave them there to stew in their own juices while I went out for a stroll.

I felt like laughing, I was happy and annoyed at all this billing and cooing between son-in-law and mother-in-law. Luckily, in a few days time we'd leave for the mountains, we'd ring in 2007 in Innsbruck, a good occasion on which to meet Marco's friends. Matteo and Sofia would also join us.

It was a New Year that will always remain in my heart. For the first time I had the chance to see Marco together with his friends. He struck me as more relaxed than he was in New York, and I discovered he was great company with a ready wit, self-confident and likeable. He knew how to take all kinds of people with grace, without ever overstepping the mark. In the evenings, when it was bedtime, he smothered me with affection and even during the day, maybe while he was doing one of his famous impersonations of Mourinho or Berlusconi, he never failed to glance in my direction. A glance that was a caress.

Sofia and I were the only ones in the group who didn't ski. During the day we strolled around downtown Innsbruck, stopped in mountain cabins or looked around the villages near the slopes as we waited for the group to return. Marco performed dangerous stunts on a snowboard, which not many people used at that time. I found out that when it came to sports, he liked to be noticed for his apparel too: a red ski suit accompanied by a brightly colored pointed woolen hat with two eye-catching pompoms. Sofia nicknamed him the pixie. I hadn't been wrong about him: he had a sunny spirit and showed his positive attitude by choosing the most unlikely color matches. Everywhere except in the office.

179

***

I have a clear memory of the morning when I decided to marry Anna. We were in our home, in New York, and I was brushing my teeth, an operation I habitually took great care over. I was flossing when she came up from behind. She was singing our song, *Il mondo* by Jimmy Fontana, and she stopped to plant a light kiss on my shoulder before disappearing beyond the doorway. It seemed like a trifle—one of those little kisses that women scatter around unsparingly to husbands, girl friends, nephews, parents...A contact with no importance and anyway, it was certainly not the first time it happened. Anna was into kissing and sometimes it irritated me when I found myself with lipstick on my cheek or nose. I couldn't understand whether she missed the target on purpose or not.

But that time her kiss had electrified me. I had to make sure I had my singing butterfly around every morning. She who always came up with something new to surprise me with.

"Breakfast is ready. Come on, we'll be late for work." Anna modulated this on the refrain of the song.

"Here I am." The vase on the table held three arum lilies; they contrasted with the gray of a day that, outside the window, threatened rain. As I was opening the jar of Nutella, I savored the effect that the decision I had just made would have.

"Why are you smiling like that?" she asked.

"Like what?"

"Like that. More than usual. Is it me or the Nutella that has this effect on you?" she laughed. "I beg you, my lord, tell me that it is I who have this effect on you. For I cannot compete with hazelnut spread."

Oh, if she only knew what I had in store for her: love, protection, care, a house for us and the children, travel, security.

Many years, each one linked to the next, a chain. We would be together forever, just like now. A fine promise modeled on the glimpse we had had of true happiness, the kind that makes you feel strong, invincible, and grants you the miracle of falling asleep and waking up beside your love.

It was cramped there at Pepita's and I wanted the best for Anna, so we moved to an apartment in Harlem. Every month we paid the rent; it wasn't cheap, and it seemed to me we were throwing money away. I began to nurse a rather crazy idea: buying a house.

"Here in New York!" Anna was astounded. We had stopped in a Starbucks for coffee. "What got that into your head?"

"I've done the accounts. We can do it."

"I'm not so sure. And where, besides?" She was so disoriented, she had forgotten her coffee.

"I've been looking around. Hey, I've got an idea of how the real estate market works."

"You're a megalomaniac." Now she was laughing. "You really do want to keep the wheels of the economy turning big time. Our economy for sure. And where should we buy a house? On Fifth Avenue?"

"Of course it's a big commitment, but I've thought of everything. Various neighborhoods are expanding, and right now the prices are still affordable. Later, when they are renovated and take off, maybe they won't be." As we made our way back home I gave her the details of my research. As I spoke, I saw her attention was growing. Anna had a passion for the real estate market; she was always up to date on the changes underway in various parts of the city, and I had often found her daydreaming over the ads in the homes for sale column. All points in my favor. It wasn't hard for me to convince her.

But the rent we're paying is already killing us." She sighed deeply.

"Problem solved."

"How?"

"We leave Harlem, make a sacrifice for a while. Go back to Pepita's."

"But..." She had a moment's hesitation. "We don't know if she can take us back. She'll have another tenant."

"That's sorted. I already called her. From the first of next month we can go back to her."

I saw her face change—her eyes grew bigger, her nostrils dilated. She stopped in the middle of the street, bent double. When she straightened up she was laughing, every so often she got her breath and yelled "You really got me there!" then started laughing again. "With the excuse of saving you're taking me back to Pepita's?"

"Are you prepared to do that?" Now I was serious. "It would be a backward step, at least for a while."

She put her arms around my neck. "What do you think? Do you think I get scared about so little?" She kissed me on the nose, as she often did, smearing me with lipstick. "Tomorrow I'll start packing up our things."

Anna was made of steel and feared nothing. She was the right woman for me, she had just proved that.

Together we would go a long way.

# 19
## MILLION DOLLAR BABY

*New York, 2008-2009*

From the day we decided we would buy a house, we devoted every free hour to the search for one that suited us. On Saturdays and Sundays we planned a round of visits to homes on offer through estate agencies. We took these commitments seriously, but we had a lot of fun, too. Occasionally a friend would come with us and then we would end the evening eating out or going to the movies or the theater.

We constantly argued about the areas from where our search should begin, but our dreams were often dashed by the limitations of our meager budget.

"Come on, Anna, let's forget it. The West Village is beyond our reach. We can't afford it." Marco scanned for the sale announcements on his tablet while I set the table for dinner. It was late, we had just got back and outside it was pouring.

"Switch on the television, please. I'm about to drain the pasta. You're right, but I love those townhouses. Did you see those wonderful red bricks, and the black and blue windows?" Marco was right. Not only the West Village, but also all of Manhattan below 96th Street was too dear for us.

"We'll find the right house soon, you'll see." He embraced me from behind, squeezing the hand in which I was holding the wooden spoon and we stirred the meat sauce together for a few seconds, then he sighed. "Now we'll limit our search to Harlem and the area just outside Manhattan. In Queens there are two interesting areas, Astoria and LIC. They're building, and sooner or later we'll have to go see," he said as he sat down. I put the dishes on the table, piping hot.

"And Brooklyn? Don't say anything," I suggested as he tried to speak with his mouth full of spaghetti. "I know that Williamsburg is already too dear, but there are also Greenpoint and Dumbo." Marco waved a hand—the television was bringing a piece of Italy into our home in the form of *Che tempo che fa*, a show we followed like a ritual. We continued eating in silence, listening to the presenter introducing Claudio Baglioni, a famous pop singer back home. But this time my mind was elsewhere. Neighborhoods and buildings ran confusedly through my head. Harlem with its tree-lined avenues, the townhouses with their stone bases, the little gardens and the steps leading up to the street doors flanked by double-hung windows. I was daydreaming. We could take a place on two floors, rent one out and use the money to amortize the cost of the mortgage. That always left the problem of reconstruction costs; much of the charm of those houses lay in the fact that they all had a story behind them. I knew that Marco wanted to buy a new house, maybe one under construction. I got a light punch on my arm.

"Hey, beautiful. Where are you?" Marco was laughing. "Aren't you watching Luciana Littizzetto? She's really on her game today."

"I'm still thinking about houses..."

"Oh boy, once you set your heart on something...We'll find the right one sooner or later." His attention went back to the show. "Did you hear that?" Marco guffawed. "Those two are really good." Meanwhile the closing theme music began to play.

The tug of war between Marco and me lasted a long time. I aimed at the houses that made me dream the most while he would bring me back down to earth by repeating the litany, *it's too dear for us*. In the meantime, months went by, we cut our spending to the bone to set aside the money necessary for such an important purchase, and we thought about finding possible new sources of income. All these sacrifices got me down a little, and because I also wanted to have fun, I would occasionally complain. He wouldn't give an inch, but he did try to motivate me. By way of an incentive to keep expenses in check he invented a game with precise rules whose results were recorded in an Excel file. The game plan was to reach the savings targets Marco had set. The more I saved, the bigger the final reward: a piece of jewelry, nothing too grand because of our limited budget, which we would buy during the summer vacation in Fano, at the jewelry store we had visited on other occasions. The prize would be to my liking, but what an effort it all was.

Every blessed day we would play our personal Monopoly, with the buildings we liked best and our personal strategies. Marco was a shrewd player, while I relied more on instinct. We felt that everything was possible. Somewhere or other our house was waiting for us, but where?

"Do you like Long Island City?" Marco called me from the office. "Do you remember I talked to you about it? But we never went. I found out that Alvin knows LIC real well."

"Good. So?"

"It's one stop from Manhattan. Let's go there today during the lunch break. Alvin's coming too, as our guide." So it was, and we immediately fell in love with the neighborhood, and the big park on the riverside that extended as far as the water taxi stop. There were lots of construction sites and we soon found the solution that suited us. Excited and enthusiastic, we made the down payment and would pay the rest with a mortgage. The house was scheduled to be ready in six months.

We were ambitious, that's for sure. We lived suspended between reality and the fanciful but not impossible prospect of attaining a goal that might change our lives. We spent a lot of our time analyzing projects that weren't entirely nutty, which would open hitherto inaccessible worlds to us.

In short, we were daydreaming.

"The formula for success can be summed up in three words: work, work, work." Marco was pragmatic even when building castles in the air.

"Ha, ha. You're impossible this evening. Look, I want to have some fun, too." I pulled his ear and he moved to one side to make me let go. He was sitting at the table amid the remains of a dinner picked up on the fly from the Chinese deli. He was looking at an Excel spreadsheet and talking seriously, but making fun of me at the same time. In fact, he was imitating a famous Italian comedian imitating Silvio Berlusconi, complete with his sibilant S.

"Come on, Anna. I know you. You're more ambitious than I am." I began clearing the table and he made me sit down. "Come here. Let's make a plan for the future."

"I don't need one. My plan is simple: to spend my life with you. All my life." Instead of the chair, I sat on his knees.

"We two have a lot in common." He poured the last drop of wine.

"Yes. We're good looking, intelligent and, above all, modest," I said ironically. I stuck my index finger under his chin and made him tilt his head back in a funny pose, like a commander. "We love each other and we'll live happily ever after. That's my fairy tale." Marco smiled at me and patted my cheek. I realized that I would never have what I wanted. At least, not right away. It was one of those times when he would become serious and get into character as a gambler. I liked to gamble, too, I loved poker, but he was playing for higher stakes, betting on our future. I unraveled his cowlick between my fingers and he, as he always did, pushed my hand away. When it came to hair he was particularly sensitive.

"You're always the same." I ruffled his hair even more energetically. "I remember that photo of you as a trainee lifeguard: red swim trunks, wooden clogs and round Prada sunglasses." He tried to get away from me as I was still pawing his hair.

"Come on, cut it out. Besides, what's that got to do with anything? It was a long time ago."

"Luckily I hadn't met you yet. I wouldn't have given you a second look with sun-bleached hair, especially knowing that you heightened the effect with chamomile shampoo. A real Fano beach boy. Get *outta* here, dude!" Now we were both laughing.

"We're provincial kids," he said, and then took on a solemn tone. "We come from modest backgrounds," he went on. "We are the youngest ones at home and with us our parents have loosened up. They've become permissive and let us have things our older brothers and sisters didn't get."

"Where are you going with this?" I didn't feel like a sermon; I still had other things on my mind. I started kissing his neck. Little, calculated kisses.

"We have goals." Marco went on, unperturbed. "We want to have a good job, to live well."

"I don't see where..." I decided I might as well move to the couch.

"Go take what you want to have." I thought the wine was beginning to take effect. The bottle of white was still on the table. Empty.

"Sure." I decided to play along with him.

"The dream, the American dream. Ours. What do you say to becoming millionaires before we're thirty?" He got up and started rummaging in a drawer. He brought a sheaf of papers to the table and started tidying them.

"Absolutely. I agree. In fact I'm sure that...What are you doing?"

"Go get your checkbook. Let's make a bet."

"What?" Now he was making out a check on the Bank of America. I tried to peek, but he withdrew.

"Well? Did you get it?" he repeated.

I ran into the bedroom, and poked around in the drawer of the bedside table. "Here it is." I went back to the living room waving the book. "What now?"

"Make out a check to yourself."

I started to laugh, thinking of my balance at that moment. "For how much?"

Marco held out his check: "Like this one," he said. The figure was for one million dollars.

I held my breath. It was electrifying just to look at a check for a million dollars, even though I knew it wasn't covered. I had joined in the game even though I still didn't know the rules.

I opened my checkbook and began to write. "Then what happens?" I was serious.

"Shall we bet that on reaching thirty at least one of us will be able to cash this check?"

"Oh, Marco." I felt like calling him a madman, yet something held me back. I signed my check and waved it in front of him without saying a word. His challenge had made me shiver, but it went away instantly.

"Now we must bless the checks." He took a bottle of prosecco di Valdobbiadene from the fridge.

"Wait. We need the right glasses," I said as I looked for the ones I had bought at the antiques market in Williamsburg.

We sealed the pact, then we put the checks in our wallets. I put mine in the same compartment in which I kept my good luck charm: a passport photo of Marco with his hair in a bowl cut.

"Now, Princess. Make sure you always carry it with you. Look at it now and then when you're angry or sad to remind yourself not to give up, even when you're happy. You'll certainly feel you can make it." Marco was crazy, sometimes bold, and even a tad cynical in business. And his madness was infectious.

"Do you think it's possible?" I whispered.

"Yes. We must have a plan, I told you that. Everything starts from there. We must make the right investments. We'll start with little things, then we'll spread our wings." All of a sudden the tension dropped and Marco burst into loud laughter. "Come on, that's enough for one evening." He put away his wallet and I did the same.

"Making sacrifices to buy a house is fine, but can we give ourselves a vacation?" It was shortly before the Fourth of July, Independence Day. I wanted to go to the seaside.

"You think we should?" Marco was stretched out on the couch, waiting for me to finish getting ready. We planned to go out to dinner with a few friends.

"I say we should. We've been working hard, we're tired. We won't go far, maybe to Mexico. Something easy. I'm ready." I came out of the bathroom. "Do I please you, my lord?" I did a pirouette that ended in a bow before him.

Marco sat up and hugged my legs and then his hands ran up beneath the skirt of my magnolia-white lined dress. He sighed: "My princess, you please me so much that I grant you the vacation. Mexico then, so be it."

Ten days after that we were lying on the beach in Tulum, baked by the sun, our skin a little reddened even though we had slathered on sunblock. It was six in the evening.

"Shall we go? I want to buy you a drink." I started to pick up our hats, beach towels and my bag.

"Wait up." Marco took the shirt he had always kept in his lap, an oddity of that afternoon. He patted it and then cautiously put it on.

"What's this about?"

"It's about looking after my things. I don't like going around all crumpled."

"Ha, ha! Mister fussbudget."

In the meantime he was ready. "After you, Princess." He bowed, placing his hand on his heart and keeping it there. I noticed this when we got to the little bar where he insisted we sit at a quiet table in the corner where the sea view was little more than a miserable wedge.

"Why here? Let's sit nearer the middle." I was already heading for another table, but he pulled my arm.

"It's fine here, trust me." It was an order.

"Are you feeling okay? Why are you keeping your hand pressed there? Does it hurt?" I was getting worried and he had an idiotic smile stamped on his face.

"Well, Marco?" The waiter came with the margaritas.

"I ordered them on coming in." I was still looking at him in puzzlement. He slipped off his chair, bent down on one knee and took a carefully folded Kleenex from his shirt pocket. "Anna, will you marry me?" Stunned, I watched as he opened up the paper handkerchief and took something out. "The box is in our room, it was too big to bring with me." He apologized as he slipped the ring on my finger.

On June 19, 2010, we got married. It was the wedding of my dreams in a castle in Tuscany, with all our relatives and close friends.

For the ceremony Marco wore a black tuxedo and I a dress with a lace-edged veil seven meters long. Both outfits were by Valentino, a wedding gift from the *maison*. Everything was perfect, as were the months before the ceremony, although they were hectic. I had my fairy tale and everything suggested it would never end.

I remember the moments together alone in the church, after the ceremony, before going out and mixing with the guests. The notes of Ennio Morricone's soundtrack to *Once Upon A Time In America* still resounded in the air, and Mom rearranged my long veil. Marco squeezed my hand and looked at my mother. "Thank you, Sveva. Thanks for everything. I wish my mother could have been here today. Luckily, you're here." All three of us looked at one another, moved, then I kissed *my husband* and held him close, without saying anything.

We went out into the churchyard, into the pandemonium of celebrations, and were inundated with rice and soap bubbles. The church door closed at our backs. The Fiat 500 in which I had arrived was waiting to take us to the reception.

A day in paradise.

But we had thousands of plans in the pipeline and, once back in New York, we got back to work, the evenings with friends at the movies or the theater, and occasional trips— sometimes with friends who came to visit us from Italy. When necessary, we lent a hand to a few young people who had followed in our footsteps and tried to make a life outside their homeland. All of them had a dream, convinced of the strength of their own worth, but some were simply weak; foolhardiness and superficiality brought them up against risks they hadn't foreseen. Nonetheless, in New York there was a good support network, and many of us offered help to those who came forward in the right way, without the safety net of connections, armed with the same enthusiasm we had had in accepting the challenge to make it on our own.

# 20
# Long Island City

The dream we had cherished for so long, to live in LIC, Long Island City, was a goal attained after many sacrifices. Finally the time had come: Anna and I were about to move into our own home.

"We've done it. I can't believe it." I was lying sprawled across the bed with arms and legs outstretched, not because I was tired and certainly not because I felt like Christ on the cross. Quite the opposite. I started to laugh, making the iPad resting on my chest wobble.

"You should calm down," Anna suggested. "We have a bunch of expenses to deal with." She was sitting beside me, with three pillows behind her back. Scattered around her were copies of *AD*, *Elle Décor* and various other design and lifestyle magazines. Her expression was serious and engrossed, but at the same time it was obvious that she was bubbling with happiness.

"Yes, come on! Let's spend. Let's make the wheels of the economy turn." I turned over onto my side and took her hand. "Anna, do you realize? We, two Italian expats in search of fortune, are colonizing our own personal piece of New York."

"You're exaggerating," she replied as she pushed the magazines away. "But we have done well," she admitted.

"We'll have to carry on working hard." I took a magazine at random and leafed through it absently. "Little by little we'll get everything done. We must be prepared for a few problems—they happen you know. The highs and lows, I mean. But..."

"What are you talking about? We've both had our share of troubles in the past." Anna turned toward me. "We've already had the bad stuff. Only nice things for Anna and Marco." She was yelling excitedly, in fact, she was euphoric. She slid down the pillows to stretch out on the bed. She was beautiful, my woman, and I liked her inside and out. I reached out my hand and caressed her from her forehead to her belly; I started to tickle her, following the line of her scars. She laughed, then she withdrew as she looked around. "You know, Marco, I can't wait to get away from here."

I followed her gaze to the red brick wall, to the dilapidated hardwood furniture, the threadbare carpet and the air conditioner, that useless old relic. The straw blinds she had put up as soon as she moved in, so as not to see the courtyard, made the room gloomy. I imagined the view from the windows of our new house: the Manhattan skyline.

We were surrounded by piles of large boxes and all around us, heaps of various things were waiting to be packed up. The bed was a raft in a sea of clutter.

"It looks like a garbage dump now," I admitted.

"It's a dream now," Anna said. "Tomorrow we're leaving. I will have good memories of this place and Pepita. If for no other reason..."

"If for no other reason than the fact that we spent our first night of non-love here." I enfolded her in an embrace.

"Yes, you snored," she said.

That evening, our last at Pepita's, we didn't have dinner. We celebrated the eve of a new life by making love.

Buying a house in LIC had cost many sacrifices and a great deal of work. We had fought hard for it, but now it was ours. Along with the mortgage.

We slept little and badly. We were in a state of excitement similar to the one I used to feel as a small boy on the day before my birthday. Waiting for the greatest present, the thing I had asked Mom for so many times that she lost patience, had been a torment. What if it didn't come? Mom always indulged me.

At dawn the drapes let in a narrow ray of light. Anna was sleeping on her back with her hair all over her face. I lay looking at her for a long time, in the half-light. The house was still silent, but the old plumbing had begun to groan its good morning.

Anna, who knows where we would go together. We had attained many goals and I had as many in the works: first there was the wedding, now the house, the green card and soon after, citizenship. I was sure we would make a few smart investments to swell the coffers, and then we would have kids. I could already see summer vacations by the sea in Italy, with a family that got bigger from year to year.

In the end I got up, trying to make no sound. I couldn't wait for the day to begin. That same evening we would sleep in the new house. I had won my first bet by making a good deal. While we waited for the house to be ready, LIC, the last neighborhood in Queens before Brooklyn, had really begun to change, to take off. While at first it had captivated us for the parks along the river and because it was full of artists and larger-than-life characters, now it was a constant blooming of stores, artisan breweries, markets, secondhand dealers and cozy bistros. And all that was only a few subway stops from Manhattan, where we worked.

My thoughts touched on our dream. The thing that...I glanced at the wallet on the bedside table, where I kept the check for a million dollars, then I stopped thinking about that. No distractions—we had a very busy day in front of us. In the meantime, I made some coffee; I would let Anna sleep for a few minutes longer. As I was fixing breakfast, I observed the room I was about to leave forever. I was daydreaming. The sunlight forced its way through the weave of the drapes and sketched on the wall what seemed like the outline of a newborn baby. I was brought back to reality by the asthmatic sound of a delivery truck that was parking to the sound of background music, maybe salsa.

"Wake up, Princess." Like every morning, I kissed the tip of her nose. For some strange reason, it was always cold, even in summer. She opened her eyes wide and looked at me without saying anything.

"Do you know where I'm taking you today? I said. "We're going to live in one of New York's trendy neighborhoods."

"Isn't that something, Marco? It's a big leap from the provincial towns where we were born. Unbelievable." She shot out of bed and onto her feet, full of unrestrainable energy. She was like a sprite. "Come on, lazybones! We've got things to do."

In that very moment someone knocked on the door: it was Pedro, a friend of Pepita's who had volunteered to work as a temporary house mover. We started to load our things onto his green stinkbug-colored truck accompanied by the sound of the radio playing Juan Luis Guerra's *La bilirrubina*. It took several trips to complete the move from Morningside Heights to LIC, but by the day's end, we found ourselves on the balcony of our new home, admiring the spectacular panorama of the park spread out at the foot of Manhattan. The huge Pepsi sign cast reddish reflections on the water of the river; on the bank, the wooden deckchairs were arranged in orderly ranks. We discovered that every evening we would enjoy a play of lights that hung in the air like a crystallized fireworks display. We sniffed at the air like dogs; the smell of newness in the apartment was inebriating. We were exhausted, but Anna wanted to immortalize the moment with a selfie focused on our smiles.

# 21
## Highs and Lows

Moving was like leaving on a new journey—life in stages. Every time we got somewhere, our enthusiasm was redoubled and produced new energy that always drove us one step farther on.

My job in finance was going well, by now I had got into the swing of things and Marco, at Valentino, had been promoted. We enjoyed our good fortune, but we didn't get swell-headed. We still liked to spread it around by assisting the young Italians who arrived here in search of their big chance. As we had done. We offered information and basic contacts, and often helped with accommodation for the first few weeks. We shared our experience with them. Besides, in the new house we had enough room to permit ourselves the luxury of having guests. We offered assistance to many people, and we learned something from them all. They also helped us make up for nostalgia, or better, the special melancholy that gets to you when you remember a face, an aroma, or a flavor that here—where there is everything—you cannot have. In their company we found the typically Italian hand gestures and the arm waving, the hugs between friends and that special familiarity that was so hard, if not impossible, to create with the locals. Those were all things that we occasionally missed, even with sorrow, on certain gray days, especially in the winter months.

Sometimes in the evenings, after eating a special dish I had prepared for him, Marco would come out with the usual joke: "An Italian woman in the kitchen and in the bedroom. These New Yorkers don't know what they're missing."

"The poor things, they always eat out and they always eat junk." I liked to encourage him. "Only yesterday I was telling a client about our Italian ritual of taking meals all together at the same table. In the end I don't think he believed me."

"Today I heard that David, you know David, still the head of marketing, has invited some people to his birthday dinner. Not us. We're not on the list, Annina."

"You know they only invite people who, for one reason or another, might be useful to them in some way."

"I know, but I'm sorry. Deep down, it makes you feel bad. For us it's so easy to be on good terms with everyone, while they are more difficult. That's not so natural. Maybe because they have no time for friendship the way we see it. We've understood that by now."

"They'll invite us when you get another promotion," I said. "Then things will take a different turn for us, too."

"Who cares? Maybe we're obnoxious." He concluded with a laugh. "We haven't heard from Fabrizio for a while." And melancholy crept in again, but we consoled ourselves by making love.

Our Italian friends were happy to visit us. We were their guides in the discovery of the country: Las Vegas, Nevada, and Arizona, where I fell in love with the Grand Canyon, and the Carolinas. We often went to Connecticut, the home of Marco's American cousins, Raymond and Connor, a branch of the Falcioni family we had discovered almost by chance, descendants of the Falcionis who had emigrated to America in the early twentieth century.

That period of our life, full of normal events, of things we liked to do and which we enjoyed in a special way, was magnificent.

On weekends, for example, we always followed the ritual of brunch; it was part of our tradition, just us two or in company. It was a moment in which we managed to put aside our worries and the tensions of the week and recharge our batteries. Sometimes we met up with friends in one of our favorite places for a lunch with blends of contrasting flavors: the sweetness of pancakes with the savoriness of bacon, coffee and prosecco, strawberries and eggs. The occasion demanded that I dress in jeans and the trendiest bomber jackets, a kind of 'brunch uniform' that was close to my heart. Marco made fun of me, but he was no better with his colorful sweaters and sunglasses from his collection. It was a game we played every now and then when we offered an Italian-style brunch at our house. Even our American friends liked my cakes, the fresh fruit I bought at the most exclusive markets, and the homemade jams that came from Italy along with some typical desserts. Sometimes brunch would last until the evening.

In summer, on Sundays we liked to take the bus to Williamsburg or even farther south, a little outside Manhattan. I felt as if we were making a journey, a one-day vacation that took us to some vernissage or a visit to the antique stores where we admired vintage modern articles, carpets, paintings, and chairs with peculiar shapes. Furniture with a history behind it enchanted us; we were fascinated by the idea of reviving old things and adapting them to our style. We tried this with a drawer unit we picked up at a pre-moving sale organized a few blocks away from our apartment. Marco worked on restoring it for several weekends, stripping the paint, sanding, and repainting it. It became the center-piece of our bedroom, the treasure chest of our most valuable and important things.

We would stroll around the Village or Chelsea, in and out of the art galleries and almost always on the way home, we would stop to buy red and yellow tulips in some Chinese deli, open night and day. At that time they were my favorite flower.

In the cold months we often went to the cinema. I remember a movie, *The Curious Case of Benjamin Button*. As the story gradually unfolded, I grew more and more distraught, and at the end I burst into tears. I couldn't help myself.

"Anna, what's the matter? It's only a movie."

"Excuse me, I can't stop. I liked it a lot. It's very poetic, but so sad. Nobody wins."

There isn't always a happy ending, in movies as in life." Marco took my arm as we followed the flow of people leaving the theater.

"I don't know what I'd do without you," I said on impulse, for no reason. He squeezed my arm and didn't reply. He was looking ahead, checking how far it was to the exit. Outside it was snowing and the contrast of the snowflakes against the neon lights blurred the outlines of the buildings, softening the edges and toning down the colors. I wasn't interested in seeing the magic of New York in this new garb. Holding Marco's arm I sank into my quilted jacket, pulled up the hood and walked with my head down and my eyes shut. I was a prisoner to a disquiet I couldn't define.

That evening I had trouble falling asleep, because I felt an infinite sadness, shot through with distress. That episode was to return to mind in the oddest moments, even when I was floating in a happiness to which I gave the color of gold.

Marco had worked his way to a great job at Valentino, he was on the way up and I was doing well, too, even though I was tired of working in finance. But all in all everything seemed perfect to me. Our life was exactly what I wanted: a harmonious progress toward the future. Over and above everything, and everyone, we were all we needed. We united body and soul to form a single energy and each of us was the other's house.

Those were wonderful years. In Italy the family was growing, and we became aunt and uncle several times over. Marco began to reveal his dreams for the future through discreet little hints: casually dropped questions about a colleague's children, an unwarranted stop in front of a window display of baby articles. I went straight on, he hung back. Signals that maybe I wasn't ready to receive, then one morning he made a suggestion: "Well, are we going to make a baby?" He understood that I wasn't ready and for a while he didn't touch on the subject again, but the respite didn't last long.

One day we were eating sandwiches in Bryant Park. The lunch break was almost over when Marco took my hands. He was wearing a serious look. "Well, when are we going to have a baby?"

"You think it's time?"

"Yes. You'd make a beautiful mother. I've been thinking about this for a long time, you know? Do you agree? Do you want to make a baby with me?" He gripped my wrists even tighter, like a chain, his tone sweet, and a caress in his eyes.

I felt unsettled. I hadn't changed a bit since we had talked about this the first time. I wasn't ready, I had my life to live. I wasn't a mother, I didn't feel like one. I would do it, of course, for him. But for a moment, I felt it was unfair.

"Sure, honey, yes. If it happens." I saw my mother and the photo of Cristina. "You know I like children. And I want one of ours, sure."

"Not *if* it happens. We'll make it happen." He let go of my hands and smiled benevolently. He checked his watch. "Heavens, it's late! I have an appointment in the office in five minutes." He kissed me and ran off. I stayed there to wander around the park for a little longer; in my mind thoughts formed and collided with one another, like bumper cars at the carnival. I started making cases, common sensical, pro-baby ones. I had to convince myself that this was the perfect moment, it wasn't reasonable to wait and I wouldn't lose my freedom or, worse, myself.

I knew I was lying.

I began to suspect that I was one of those women who never find the right time to become a mother.

It had to happen to me, like an accident. Only that way would it go well.

An end that would be a new beginning.

We started to try.

Sometimes I thought that making love wasn't the same. The feeling you're doing it because you have to produce a result.

Your body no longer serves for love and pleasure.

You become a body useful for reproduction.

You are no longer you. You doubt.

Your life, your plans.

But it's nice to think of a child.

There would be three of us. Three and then, maybe, four.

Names: I had chosen Margherita and Tommaso, Marco liked Annamaria and Raffaele. After some effort we reached a compromise on Valentina and Alessandro. They would have my ears and Marco's smile.

For a while there was no change of direction in my life, everything was proceeding regularly; every month the certainty that nothing was going to change. The end of twenty-eight days was always what counted.

We tried for more or less two years and nothing happened.

We wanted it so badly. In the end I wanted it too, maybe because it was such a long time coming. We needed to try something and I'm a meticulous type. It wasn't a torment, at least not for me, but it was a thorny issue. An obsession, disguised by the idea of a principle: the real proof of a woman's love for her man.

As life went on as usual, I began a series of medical tests in order to get the in-vitro fertilization procedure underway. There was no anxiety about having to undergo a medical examination to check out the chances of procreation. Or at least, I didn't feel anxious. Maybe I was confused by the fact that I wasn't totally captivated by the idea of motherhood. During the whole time we tried to have a baby, there had been moments when I had wondered why I was taking part in the project with such detachment.

I pondered, I reasoned, but I never delved into the matter too deeply. I didn't want to know myself from that standpoint. Veiled guilty feelings stopped me from doing that, yet, if I had gotten pregnant, I would have been glad. For Marco.

We women are always torn between ourselves and someone else.

In the meantime, I was planning to change jobs, to set up a business that would give me more independence. At the top of any New Yorker's wish list was a wedding in Italy, provided she could afford it. And I intended to make that wish come true. I would have to fly to Italy to assess my chances of setting up a partnership as a wedding planner.

"You realize this could work? You've had a great idea. Let's see what you need to get started..." Marco was enthusiastic.

We got into the part as entrepreneurs. The idea of tackling a project with an element of risk as well as a great chance of success excited us. Both of us still kept the famous check for a million dollars in our wallets. The deadline for the bet, reaching the age of thirty, was getting close. I booked a flight to Rome. This challenge had taken my mind off the idea of a baby. Marco brought me back to the notion.

"By the way, the hospital called today. The investigative procedure calls for a series of tests for me, too, and then I'll have to donate my precious sperm."

"How will you manage without me?" I laughed, then grew serious again. "I wonder why they always test you men second, and us women first?" I complained. "This prejudice, this idea that the problems are always due to us women irritates me." He pulled my arm and sat me down on his knees.

"Be not angered, my princess. I beg of you!"

"I am not the princess, I am the queen. The queen of America." I feigned disdain, and he started kissing me on my neck and behind my ears.

"Oh, my prince!" I sighed. "Will you manage to do without me for a few days?"

"I'll miss you, Anna," he replied seriously, then he started kissing me again.

The next day I left for Italy to assess the feasibility of my wedding planning project.

One week later, around midday, the phone call came.

"Hi, sweetheart. I wish you were here with me. I'm in San Gimignano, in Piazza della Cisterna, it's..."

"Anna," Marco said only my name. His voice was like a taut wire.

"What's the matter?" I pricked up my ears. "What's happened?"

"Don't worry. Everything's under control. You know, the tests...When the doctor read my medical history..." I heard him gasp and I was instantly afraid.

"Come on, Marco, spit it out!" Now his hesitation was rattling me. I felt a stab of headache. "Tell me."

"When he heard that I had had Wilms tumor as a child, he prescribed a scan. Just in case, he said. I thought he was being overly scrupulous—I've always been well. Anyway he set the test for yesterday. I went to it unworried, I really wasn't thinking about it and during the scan, not immediately, but a few minutes after it had begun, the technician apologized and went out. That's never a good sign."

I slumped down onto the steps of the well in the center of the square. I could sense that Marco was trying to control his concern. I had no need of further confirmation, I clamped icy fingers around the telephone. Desperation is cold.

"Anna, they've found a nephroblastoma in my kidney. It's come back." Now that he had gotten this off his chest he was calmer. At least it seemed that way from his tone of voice. In New York it was early morning, and Marco would have certainly spent a sleepless night.

"Where are you?" I asked.

"At the office, but I got in early. I'm alone. I don't want anybody to know. At least for the time being." I imagined him sitting at his desk, the phone in one hand, while the other tugged remorselessly at his earlobe. Almost certainly he was wearing one of his elegant lead gray suits, a pale blue shirt... A handsome man, young and full of life, smart. My man.

"There must be a cure. Have they already decided what to do?" The headache was now concentrated behind my eyes. I had a bitter taste in my mouth and I felt the wind had been knocked out of me.

"Chemotherapy, for sure. It'll be tough." A pause. He was expecting comfort from me. I was terrified; I didn't know what to say. I was struck by a thought: the idea of the baby was shelved, at least for now. I wanted to go ahead with my life with Marco. Us two. It had all been so beautiful until that moment!

We remained silent for too long. The first to regain control of the situation was Marco, who even tried to make a joke, "Look, Anna, I managed it anyway. Even without you. I made it. The sperm, I mean." He wanted to cheer me up. "Now it's safe. Frozen."

"Why didn't you call me right away, yesterday?"

"So as not to hurt you," he said in a whisper. "I know you were doing okay. Until ten minutes ago you were happy, weren't you? Now because of me..."

"Please! We'll get through this. Marco, how do you feel?"

"Never better, my love." He seemed on the verge of tears. That wasn't like him.

"I'm booking a flight. I'm coming straight home."

"There's no need. I'll get by. Listen to me, finish what you have to do." He gave a deep sigh.

"No. I'm coming home. I want to be there with you."

Once more we fell silent for a few seconds, I figured he was trying to compose himself, then he said, "Then I'll wait for you, sweetheart." He hung up.

# 22
## STAGE FOUR

*New York, April 2012*
That was it. I had told her.

I would never have wanted to hurt Anna, but there was no way I could avoid telling her. And it wouldn't have been right to delay the announcement. I knew her—she would have been too hurt.

Telling Anna I had cancer had drained all my energy—I was worn out, confused. Above all, I had no more certainties. My thoughts, my plans, the thousands of things I had in the works, everything had been swept away when they gave me the diagnosis.

I needed to get used to the idea of cancer inside me; I visualized it as a cockroach stuck to my kidney, the only one I possessed because the tumor I had had at eighteen-months-old had carried off the other one. So I had already paid my dues, yet that wasn't enough. Not yet. What was it? Fate, bad luck, a punishment for god only knows what, the burden of the world's sins that someone had to carry, pollution, the genetics of a defective DNA, the discontent that sometimes bubbled up in me, unjustified, like a feeling of ingratitude for a life that was good in any case, the unease of knowing I was not doing enough? Enough in what sense?

For whom? Ambition, maybe too much ambition? Wanting more and more. Why?

Misfortune's wheel had turned and had stopped on me. This was a fact.

I was exhausted and I had to start fighting. The office was still deserted, but from somewhere in the corridor I could hear the cleaners moving around. I wasn't ready to meet other people.

Maybe walking would calm me down and allow me to gather my thoughts more rationally. I left the office and headed for Bryant Park. It was a beautiful spring day; the colors were brighter than usual, with people's faces seeking the sun, many of them wearing smiles even though they were alone. I decided to go to the Lilac Bar, as Anna called it on account of the color of the sign and the décor. I sat at a table from where I could see the bench on which Anna I and usually sat. Now it was free, or rather, empty.

Devoid of the two of us.

How many ideas we had shared sitting there, and how many kisses. Even arguments.

I hadn't told her everything. For example, I had not mentioned the fact that the disease had been classified as being stage four. I would let her know when she arrived; it would be impossible to avoid telling her.

She had to know. Only her.

I would decide on the scenario. I didn't want to be pitied, treated like an invalid, with too much attention, or like an outcast because anyway...I wanted to live a full life as long as that was possible. The chemotherapy would knock me flat. But in the end it would save me, maybe.

'Shit, and then I'm going to get through this. I'm so young!' These thoughts were clamoring inside my head as the waiter set down the coffee and the slice of pie I had ordered out of habit. I discovered that I was unable to swallow. I carefully broke up the pie and then began to scatter it around, throwing the pieces as far as I could toward the grass. In one minute a splash of quivering feathers formed in the green of the grass. Among the many birds assembled for the banquet, I thought I spotted Anna's blackcap, the one that started hanging about her in March and later came up with no fear to take the crumbs from her hand.

Around me everything was as it always was, better than always because it was a beautiful day; the background hum of the city ebbed and flowed depending on the intensity of the traffic.

Spring is a happy season.

April. A memory made its way to the surface. Back home they said it was April when I got sick the first time, as a baby. They got the diagnosis on Good Friday. 'Records of information should be controlled.' Another odd thought. It was important to decide who I should share the news with. Anna: done already, and besides, she was me.

My brother Matteo, Sofia, but no one else at home. Not my father nor my aunts and uncles and far less other relatives and friends. Those who loved me would worry and anyway, it served no purpose. They lived far away, and we wouldn't know what to say to one another. Our relationships would change, or worse, the effort of finding the right words to say to me would put them off. Too much embarrassment. I would lose contacts and friendships out of too much affection—not everyone has enough courage to share suffering. Even though you are important to them, they can't handle it, I already found that out when my mother died. At school some kids had looked at me in silence, distant, with an uneasiness bordering on fear on their faces. The mere idea that it could happen to them too, to suddenly lose their mother, crushed them. They stayed away from me out of caution, not indifference.

I understood. If you're an adolescent busy discovering the world, you can't conceive of the grief I found myself swimming in. Everyone was fond of me, but my classmates and the others avoided me so as not to be affected by the enormity of my pain.

Now the same thing would happen. Sharing the information with too many people would help no one.

Anna, my brother and Sofia would not let me feel sorry for myself. We would get through this, we could count on our strength; nothing else was needed.

I was going to carry on living a normal life.

Normal?

I would feign my normality in order to carry on enjoying that of others. It would help me to go on.

And anyway, I could make it. I *would* make it.

Stage four: spread to the extra-abdominal lymph nodes.

The chemotherapy would wear me down to a frazzle. I would hang in there because I wanted a life similar to my normal one.

I could make it.

Stage four.

The thoughts were running around my head, always the same ones.

Anna would arrive tomorrow.

I paid the check and headed off toward the office. I felt heartened. I entered the cone of shadow cast by the skyscrapers. Instinctively I looked for the blue of the sky up there, beyond the buildings. I bumped into a baby carriage. I apologized and had just enough time to glimpse the round face of a newborn baby. The mother walked on and with that unknown woman, the scene I had dreamed of so many times faded away. I, Anna, and our two children, a boy and a girl, strolling here in Bryant Park and then in Italy, by the sea: the sandcastles, the waves, and swimming all together.

# 23
## BALANCED ON WINGS

I have always been afraid of the deep, rolling rumble of steel cutting through the air, slashing the sky. On every take off I shrink back, trying to sink into the padding of my seat.

My heart... Amid that din I could hear it beating to a more and more frenzied rhythm. I was sweating.

In the plane, the imperfect silence that accompanies every take off made me anxious. The little coughs, the throat clearing, a sigh so deep it spread through the rows of seats, the murmur of fragmented conversations as they died away. All this was proof of how much the moment of take off was a thought lurking in everyone's mind. When the strained howl of the engines dropped to a regular tone, I drew a breath and my color returned.

The display announced that we could remove the safety belts as the flight attendants began to pass around the cabin.

"Everything okay?" The flight attendant gave me a reassuring smile. Maybe she had noticed my pallor.

"Yes, thanks." I got more comfortable in my seat as she observed me with an expert eye. "I've flown a lot, but I'm always afraid. It's something I just can't beat." I smiled and looked around as if I were curious; I needed to take my mind off things. She nodded and proceeded along the aisle.

Beneath me the Venetian lagoon unfolded, shrouded in mist. Land and sea in gray.

The colors were the same as my first flight to New York, in 2001, a trip organized by the school. I had left the Big Apple for Canada the day before the attack on the Twin Towers. I remember my parents' voices over the telephone, desperate. I didn't understand. I couldn't believe that it had happened only just after my departure. The idea that perhaps I had avoided death by a matter of hours left me stunned. There, where I was, I followed the guided tours and the study sessions like an automaton. I was outside my group of friends; I was detached, alone, alive but somehow not quite in myself. Dragged into a vortex of homesickness I couldn't escape from. Just like now, only now in order to get back home I had left Italy and flown to New York.

This time, too, the news had come over the telephone. A shock.

It was cold on the plane. I loosened my jacket, huddled down and closed my eyes. The Xanax was taking effect, fortunately. Maybe I wouldn't need anything else.

"Annabeola, Annabeola...where are you?" My brother Raffi was looking for me in the yard while I was hidden in the house, behind the kitchen door. We were playing hide and seek and I, even though I was the younger, always managed to fool him. I had slipped indoors while Mom was hanging up laundry in back. He counted out the time, slowly reeling off the numbers. By the time he got to eight I was already hidden. I had also managed to get hold of the Nutella jar and now, well hidden, and I was pulling out long tongues of chocolate spread with my fingers. My brother was still looking for me. "Annabeola, Annabeola..." Inside, the fragrance of fresh laundry blended with the aroma of coffee; for me it was the scent of some exotic sweet treat. Good.

An air pocket brought my thoughts—still immersed in hazelnut spread—back to the surface. I was no longer a little girl, I was alone as I flew over the ocean and I was afraid. The fact that I was in an airplane had nothing to do with it. I was afraid for Marco, Marco and me. It wasn't panic yet, but a feeling of angst that had seeped through the chinks in my armor; it ruined my desire to feel good, in peace, as I had been before the phone call, when my world, our world, was going right. Everything in its place: love, work, plans, friends, travel.

The future within reach.

I started to roll up a lock of hair with my fingers; I pulled it until it hurt, then let it go before starting to turn it into an artificial curl again. My mother would have shot me black looks to tell me to stop, then she would have given me a little slap on the hand. Instead, I was free to torture my hair. My mom was at home, maybe rinsing the salad or making the bed. Maybe she was feeding the cat. I was certainly in her thoughts and as she thought of me, she hugged me tight.

I suddenly let go of the lock of hair between my fingers.

"Do you want to be curly?" Marco would have laughed. If we'd been in bed he would have taken my wrist between his teeth, delicately, like a dog seeking its master's attention.

Marco. The phone call, a hint of suffering.

Maybe it was just a change of pace, a stop. We would slow down and then get underway again. I felt even colder. 'All I need is a blanket,' I thought. 'Everything will work out.'

I gave myself a smile to bolster my courage. I wanted, I *had* to get back in control, but I was confused, stunned. Usually so rational and organized, for once I was struggling to find my fighting spirit. I took off my glasses and my surroundings appeared blurred, people's faces took on fuzzy outlines just as the edges of the seats dissolved into one indistinct mass. I was distancing myself from the reality that awaited me and that I still didn't know. There was nothing good about it.

Stupid of me, I shouldn't have even thought that. I imagined Marco, his confident smile, the one he reassured me with about everything when he told me that things would be okay. He made me feel good, and with him I was always at home. Alone with him.

I remembered his voice over the phone, hesitant. Stammered syllables, quavering words, a subdued tone.

It wasn't good.

I moved my legs and tried to get more comfortable. I felt like running and yelling and maybe even breaking something. Since the phone call, I had always been in the company of others, forced to be polite and measured, while I was trying to repress the nausea that assailed me from time to time. Like now.

It would have been good for me to get my mind off things, to chat. That wasn't like me—usually I'm reserved—but in that moment I was full of emotions I couldn't contain. I would have liked to run away from myself, have a respite. I nodded off, slipping back into my memories.

I was wide-awake the first time Marco explained to me that we were fated to be together, even in our imperfections. He used to repeat that often and each time he would run his fingers over the scar that ran across my belly—the *track*, he called it. And he used to pretend he was pushing the wagon of a toy train running gently over the welt left by my accident with his index and middle fingers. His scar was less marked, and also less recent than mine, but it was there. The signs of past suffering united us. They told us we had gotten over bad things, that we had had our share and didn't have to fear the future.

It wasn't true. The phone call was proof of that.

A thought started to pound like a hammer in my head: I didn't know where I was going. If all went well, knock on wood, I would arrive in New York, but my true *where* was Marco, and Marco...God, I didn't want to even think of it. What was this? A new beginning? The continuation of something? Life can be seen in many ways. Maybe I could just breathe and that's all. No, that was ruled out.

I would face everything with Marco. They would treat him—New York has the best doctors in the world. I imagined him in a hospital bed, me at home, alone in rooms left lackluster by his absence, and then...

Then he would come home.

The attendant from before was in front of me again, with the cart smelling of lousy coffee, croissants, fake orange juice, salami...The whole thing disgusted me.

"Would you like something?"

"How much longer?" I asked.

"A little less than five hours."

'God, still far too long!' I thought. "Some water, please." A half tablet of lorazepam would help me get over the ocean.

The last thing I thought before sinking into an artificial sleep was that no one would take Marco from me—he was mine. A few hours later I went through the airport checks repeating the same concept to myself over and over. I wanted to believe that my wish would come true. I clung to the idea that if I willed Marco's recovery with all my might, then he would be cured. I decided I would make a vow, actually two: no more chocolate and not even new shoes until they said he was well again. A childish thing, I knew, but I felt it was important. I clenched my fists and narrowed my eyes as I swore to myself that I would honor my pledge.

Marco was waiting for me with his usual smile and relaxed air. We hugged without saying a word.

"How was your flight? Were you very scared?"

"I took a pill," I replied with a sniff. "You look good." The words came out just like that, without any intention.

"Sure, I'm just fine." He laughed quietly. He was in a good mood and that reassured me. In the cab he took my hands, caressing them and kissing my fingertips. "I feel good because you've arrived. Nothing has changed. We have a problem and we'll solve it."

"Everything will be fine. Have you done any research on the net?" I immediately regretted having asked that.

"No," he said hastily, and I knew he was lying.

"When are we going to the doctor?"

"Monday. I'm going alone, no need for you to waste your time."

"I'll have all the time I need. I'm through with finance and I'm going to change my job. I've thought it over carefully and I've made up my mind. I've always wanted to be a real estate agent, you know. This is the right moment. I'll have more time for us. We can be together more often. As for my projects in Italy...let's shelve them for a while."

He looked at me pensively as he rummaged through his pockets, "You must think it over carefully." Eventually he found his sunglasses, put them on and turned to look out of the window.

We got to Queens and the cab began the climb toward the point where the panorama of the New York skyline opens out. I kept silent. This was the place, the moment in which, upon returning from a trip, we finally felt we were home. A minute later Marco sank back in the seat, close to me. He wanted my warmth, my protection; now he was the one looking for a home. I had to give him courage, I knew this was a special moment and I was stricken by fear.

I was with him and I was alone. When the cab pulled over in front of our door I gathered my strength to make an attempt at being cheerful.

"Do we have any food in the fridge?"

Marco was paying the driver, and he looked up in surprise: "I didn't think to get anything."

"Shall we go out then? You surely don't want your princess to starve to death?" My acting was not very good. He didn't reply, but took my suitcase and followed me into the lobby and then into the elevator. We smiled, a little embarrassed. I turned to kiss him before slipping the key in the lock, and his response was distracted, distant.

I switched on the light. The hospital documents were scattered all over the table, along with the images of the scan.

"Excuse me. I had forgotten about them." He started to gather up the papers. I headed for the bathroom and as I shut the door behind me, the tears had already begun to flow.

I felt things had changed.

I turned on the faucet in the sink. The flow of our life had changed course. 'We'll have a tough period. Difficult days lie ahead, but we're young and we'll pull through.' I dried my tears and fixed my makeup. I put my ear to the door. I was sure Marco had been weeping too and I didn't want to take him by surprise. Like me, he needed time to compose himself. I stayed with my ear glued to the wood for a couple of minutes, then I opened the door. I was halfway along the hall when the apartment was filled with a melody I knew well.

> No, last night my love
> I wasn't thinking of you anymore
> I've opened my eyes
> To look around me

It was Jimmy Fontana's *The World*. The volume was very loud.

> And around me
> The world is turning as it always does
> It turns, the world turns
> In boundless space

Marco came toward me. He was wearing an apron with a picture of a piping hot pizza on the bib. He began to sing along as he took my hand, inviting me to dance.

> Where love has just begun
> Where loves are already ended
> With the joy and the pain
> Of people like me
> O world
> Only now, as I look at you
> I get lost in your silence
> And I'm nothing beside you

"You're crazy. Turn the music down. You'll get us kicked out!" We danced until the song ended and he turned down the volume on the radio.

"When I heard them playing our song I couldn't resist. I said to myself it was a good omen." He dragged me into the kitchen where the water was boiling on the stove. "Now I know. Everything's going to be all right."

"Marco, listen..."

"For this evening let's not talk about it anymore. I'm going to cook the spaghetti now. I'll see to everything. You're tired after the journey."

"No, I'm not!" I protested.

"Yes, you are. Tonight only cuddles for my queen of New York." He laughed, but his eyes were moist.

From the next day I started researching the tumor on the net, both on American and Italian sites. Marco had been very unlucky, that form was really rare in adults. But we were going to fight, and knowing the enemy made us feel stronger.

I got started on the paperwork required to become a licensed realtor. Marco told his brother and I told my mother. It was hard and sad. We felt guilty about the suffering we were inflicting on the people who loved us most.

We were desolate. We pretended that everything was as usual. A way to survive a misfortune that, as the days gradually went by, seemed too great to bear.

Good moments and bad, sun and rain, white and black.

The doctor who was helping Marco with the legal procedures for in vitro fertilization and who had found the tumor, passed our case on to Dr. Barbara Flores, an Italian-Argentinean oncologist who we liked straight off and who made us feel we were in good hands. She prescribed Marco a hospital visit for further tests. We had top-quality health insurance and we could afford the best: a five-star hospital. We had found our general, Dr. Flores, lined up our troops and stocked up on munitions. I was certain we would win.

# 24
## THE EDGE OF LIFE

Anna's strength and optimism were infectious and, thanks to her, I took heart. Yet my life swung between awareness and numbness, amid an unhealthy lassitude filled with incoherent thoughts. One moment I felt sure I was going to make it, even downplaying my illness as if ignoring it were enough to make it go away; the next moment I felt crushed by the enormity of what happened to me, aware of the scant prospects of a cure offered by the treatment I was undergoing. I tried hard to stay within the bounds of an uncertain equilibrium and clung to the repetition of my day-to-day routine, hour after hour. I concentrated on the immediate necessities of work or whatever else was capable of taking my mind off things.

I was playing a part, and keeping faith with the character I had chosen gave me an illusion of strength. This thing, this serious illness that leaves no way out and always happens to someone else, had happened to me. It was a fact I accepted from a distance, with detachment.

They had given me a term, an indication of a limit: maybe five years. A span of time in which I would find my solution. Perhaps some researcher's discovery would save me, otherwise, I would spend the evening of my life in the best possible way. With Anna.

In the meanwhile, she had got busy straight away and, once she got her realtor's license, she started her new job. I remember how excited she was, even happy at times, despite me. I watched her get ready, carefully choosing the right outfit, the high heel shoes, the shade of red for her lips. In some ways, a new job can arouse the same excitement as a passionate love affair. I envied her that future, for her alone, that had no expiration date and, of course, I was also very happy for her. I supported her especially when the difficulties of a profession that requires you to navigate in an ocean full of madmen and sharks emerged in all their complexity.

At first it was very hard, but Anna pulled out her habitual determination to succeed. She had always been tenacious, but working as a real estate agent in New York is the toughest test. Her appointments were set for the oddest times with all kinds of people, dealing with some of whom took all her patience. Sometimes it went well, sometimes not. It took her a while to make any headway, but she never gave up. When she felt down after an appointment had gone badly I would console and encourage her. I was sure she would make it even when she came home exhausted, her eyes veiled with tears of anger or discouragement and, instead of winding down, she would ask me for my 'medical bulletin.' That was what we called, in jest but not too much so, the daily account of examinations, tests, and medicines taken. When there was some news she would go deeper into it by researching the net and then sending results and opinions to certain experts, cancer specialists in Bologna with whom we had set up a kind of ongoing online consultation.

The medical front dispensed with, we would try to comfort each other and look to tomorrow. As time gradually went by, our weekly dinner dates, theater shows and meetings with friends grew less frequent, replaced by all that my treatment involved. Some evenings we took refuge on the couch, locked in a gentle embrace and murmuring snippets of conversation.

"How are you feeling, darling?" Anna asked. "We have chemo tomorrow morning, I'll come with you."

I was silent for a bit, then I said: "Okay, but weren't you supposed to go to Tribeca?"

"In the afternoon. Latish. We've plenty of time."

Between us there was cancer, a limited future and work, which was important for Anna now, more than it was for me. There were also all those things that stand on the finish line of a normal life: payments, vacations, anniversaries, even gossip and the faulty washing machine we needed to change, and the need to get life in order. We didn't mention this, mainly out of fear, shame and respect, because facing certain problems would have lent substance to a future we rejected.

During the times we still went out with friends, either to dinner or the theater, life went on almost as it always had, but my desire to do such things waned. I gradually began to hide inside myself, without letting it show. I don't think even Anna realized this.

I withstood the cycles of chemo well, and I managed to follow a routine that was almost regular. It was mere appearance. The space around me grew pokier with every passing day. The hospital seemed smaller every time I went in. Being in any kind of medical environment gave me a feeling of constriction that I struggled to deal with and to conceal from Anna. Every so often I noticed that she was staring at me, her eyes full of unspoken questions. Maybe I was sitting on the gurney in my floral hospital gown and colored cap and she was standing in front of me, elegant and perfect, stunning as ever; she was ready to go out, toward life, to be swallowed up by the frenetic rhythm of the city, while I measured out my time by the infusion of drugs or counting the minutes closed up in the tunnel of the MRI scanner.

# 25
# YOU DON'T WANT TO UNDERSTAND

My mother and Marco's brother Matteo made the flight together. Instead of giving me comfort, their arrival made my distress even more acute. At the airport I was the only one waiting to meet them since Marco was doing chemo. We hugged for a long time, our eyes moist, then I rebelled and recoiled.

"It's not right. There's no need for tears. Marco is following the course of treatment. He'll get better like he did the first time, as a baby." I took my mother's suitcase. Matteo squeezed my elbow and smiled. We set off, a trio thrown off balance by the weight of too many worries.

"My brother is strong. Sofia keeps on telling me that, too. He's bound to come out of this well, he's going to beat this terrible thing." He cut through the crowd and looked around curiously. "What a shambles. I really couldn't stay here." I made a few wisecracks in reply while I observed my mother. She didn't speak nor did she listen to what we were saying. She had aged since I saw her last; her cheeks were sagging and lots of little lines had appeared around her mouth. She reminded me of certain photographs of my grandmother.

"Everything okay, Mom?"

"Yes. When's Marco coming back?"

"In the late afternoon." In the meantime we had come to the cabstand. Matteo was making sure the driver put all the baggage in the trunk.

"We'll have time to talk," she whispered. "Alone."

"Is everything okay at home?" I asked as I held the door open for her.

"Didn't I tell you? Your brother has a new girlfriend. Maybe she's the one." She was good at changing the subject, and manipulating people, too. When we got to our house she managed to persuade Matteo to go to Marco at the hospital, without even giving him time for a little rest after the journey. The two brothers would keep each other company.

I put her things away in a heartbeat, but not before having dusted the guest room I had prepared specially for her. Matteo would sleep on the couch in the living room.

Eventually she sat down at the kitchen table in front of a cup of steaming hot coffee. She had brought the blend from Italy. "Sit down, Anna." She didn't drink the coffee straight off—it was still too hot. I noticed the pearl pink nail polish, her favorite, her hair tinted at the last moment before leaving, and her nails almost intact thanks to an extra dose of lacquer. Her outfit was new; I hadn't seen it before.

"A good thing I'll be here for a while. I'll give the house a quick once over." She looked around with a suspicious air.

"Do you think some animal is going to creep out from under the couch?" I was making fun of her—she was obsessive about cleaning.

"You have to look after your husband." Her attention was on me once more and she gave me a sorrowful look that made me feel like crying again. I gritted my teeth.

"I do nothing else, what do you think!" I got up to look for the cakes I had bought specially for her. Now I was the one who needed something tasty that might console me, so I took a cream horn.

"I've gone into this. I'm sorry, child. You don't want to understand, I know."

"If you've come here just to talk this way, you can go straight back to Italy." I had never spoken to my mother like that. I was on the point of screaming at her that she was a bitch. I, who was so very close to and respected her. It was our first fight since the one many years before, when I had told her I was in love with Marco. I jumped to my feet, wiped the cream off my fingers with a paper napkin, balled it up and threw it in the sink. I stood leaning against the kitchen counter, turning my back on her. "Don't say anything else. It would be too much." I wished she had never come.

"Listen, child, we won't have many chances to be alone. Listen to me now. Only a miracle can get Marco out of this. I believe in miracles. And I pray for him every morning and every night. But there's no guarantee. Look after him. And drop your obsession with work. Take some time and be with him. It's not that you *have* to do this, quite the contrary. But in case...after...afterward you would have no remorse. Do you see, child?"

I had turned my back on her, I couldn't restrain my anger. I felt like I hated her. I folded my arms and clenched my fists as a bubble of air rose up from my stomach, expanded in my esophagus and pushed. To get out.

"Anna!" she cried, to shake me out of it. I grabbed my jacket and bag without looking at her and ran out. When I got to the street I went down to the subway and got into the tail-end car. I rode up and down for a few stops, squeezed up amid the crowd. At least there I could be in peace and cry alone. The stampede to get on and off the car, the hiss of the pump that controlled the sliding doors, the smell of dirt and expensive perfumes, the sound of handbags, briefcases and plastic and paper bags brushing against legs. My tears didn't stop flowing. But no one looked me in the face. I was free to pity myself, to suffer for Marco. In the mid afternoon off-peak hours the crowd began to thin out. I still hadn't stopped crying, my blurred eyes fixed on the metal clasp of my bag, my contracted fingers opened and closed the butterfly snap. I had run out of tissues, but that didn't matter. I looked up and met the gaze of a black woman sitting opposite me. Forty at most, she was wearing a pink overcoat with light gray shoes and handbag. She was very elegant, a good-looking woman whose dark face was furrowed by two iridescent tracks. I had never realized that tears are more noticeable on a black face. I felt that in some way we shared some great grief. I got up and when I passed in front of her I nodded. At my stop I got out and walked slowly back to my door.

Marco had worried about me, too. A few years before, I had suffered with a kidney stone. The pain had begun at the office, at first it was bearable, then it increased to the point that I decided to call him.

"I'm sick," I whispered into the telephone. "Come get me. I want to go home." He rushed over there and found me bent double with pain.

"Wouldn't it be better to go straight to the hospital?" He asked as he got me into the cab, handling me with the maximum care.

"No. It'll go away now. Don't make me speak." He gave our address to the  driver. All I remember of that ride was catching occasional glimpses of the driver looking at me. He was observing me in the rear-view mirror, maybe he was afraid I would mess up the car; numbed with pain, I looked back at him, mesmerized by the network of lines on his face. It looked like the map of Manhattan complete with bridges.

As soon as I got home I took refuge on the couch.

"What can you take?" I heard Marco rummaging in the medicine cabinet in the bathroom. "Tylenol? What do you take for your period?"

"I took all kinds of stuff in the office. I'm sure this has nothing to do with my period." I realized that my voice was shrill. An even stronger stab of pain made me cry out.

"I'm taking you to the hospital," he said. In the meantime, he touched my forehead and felt my wrist, pressing his index and middle finger just below my palm. Everything irked me; I was suffering.

"You're running a temperature," he said. "It could be appendicitis."

"Let's wait a little longer." By that time I was gasping. He was already on the telephone, giving our address. We lived in Harlem then. The ambulance arrived a few minutes later. Marco stayed with me the whole time, holding my hand and stroking my hair and the outline of my face. He reassured me.

In the emergency room they immediately hooked me up to a drip. I slipped into unconsciousness from which I emerged some hours later, exhausted, but with no more pain. After the appropriate medical tests, the crisis was overcome and with a diagnosis of kidney stones, they discharged me. A nurse took me to the elevator in a wheelchair. Marco was waiting for me there. "You look like hell," I said, pretending to be scandalized.

"And you're beautiful, right?" Finally, after hours, we managed to laugh again. "I haven't moved from here, you know."

"You didn't go home?" Now we were in the lobby. A stream of people was coming and going, and he stopped right there in the middle of the room and bent over to kiss me on the neck. A tender kiss, which moved me.

"Let's go." He pushed the chair again. "Both of us need a shower." Marco took me home and when I came out of the bathroom, he made me go to bed. He fixed me a light snack and gave me the medicines, then he lay down next to me. I remember that I was on my back and he was stretched out on his belly with one arm across my chest as with his hand behind my neck he gently stroked my hair.

"Don't do that ever again," he said.

"Do what?" The quiet of the bedroom was made even more intimate by the hum of the heating. I liked that sound, warm in every sense.

Marco came even closer and rubbed his nose against my cheek. "I felt lost. There was nothing I could do to take away your pain. I wished it was mine, instead of watching you suffer like a dog." His eyes were gleaming; he drew back from me and sniffed. "I couldn't live without you," he muttered.

Still absorbed by that memory I loved so much, I had arrived at my front door. I hesitated; it was almost time to eat. Marco and his brother would soon be back, my mother would certainly be bustling about in the kitchen and maybe she had begun the spring-cleaning. I wasn't going to give her the chance to go back to the subject we had broken off so rudely. I cursed the fact that I wasn't alone with Marco. Do relatives come to give comfort? They speak their minds instead, saying things you don't want to hear, truths you could do without.

I loved my mother and Matteo loved his brother, but Marco and I had the right to be alone on our island. I realized that now that we had been invaded.

We were living within the margin of time that medicine guaranteed us because that space was a certainty and there were no arguments. For me, *after* wasn't even on the horizon, my gaze had shrunk to boundaries beyond which I imagined nothing.

# 26
# A HAND OF POKER

*New York, December 2012*

Both Marco and I distanced ourselves from Christmas as soon as the city started to dress up for the holidays. Without saying anything to each other and without any immediate cause for alarm, we preferred to live in a tranquil climate, far from the excesses of parties, flavors, sounds, and crazy spending that Christmas had always brought us. Whereas in previous years we liked to keep the radio tuned in to the channel that constantly played *Last Christmas, Rockin' Around The Christmas Tree, So This Is Christmas* and other similar songs, now we avoided it and we also limited our appearances at the many parties before the holidays. We were uneasy, each of us concealing a trace of unhappiness from the other. On the outside we were both clad in a veneer of relative serenity, but time was becoming our enemy. I sensed this from certain prolonged absences when Marco went for medical consultations. He would use an excuse to avoid my attending the most important appointments. Marco didn't want me with him in order to shield me from the toughest verdicts, preferring to take them on his own. And he no longer sensed my wishes because he was concentrating on himself, and that was right: he was fighting for his life.

Nothing was as it had been before, but we could have cheated by getting out of there, fleeing from that oppressive everyday routine. I realized that I didn't want to spend the last days of the year waiting for something that we would never have wanted to see arrive.

We had already given up our usual trip to Italy, so as not to spend Christmas with the family. The few who knew about it, my parents, Matteo and Sofia, had done everything to persuade us to change our minds, but we had stood firm. We didn't want to find ourselves all together at tables laden with all manner of good things surrounded by people, every one of whom would feign a false serenity. At first we had decided to stay in New York, but now that no longer suited me. The festive atmosphere had never seemed so phony to me.

"We need a vacation," I said a few days before Christmas.

"Do you want to go away? Where?" I thanked heaven that Marco hadn't replied saying that he didn't feel like it, and I took this as a good sign.

"Let's play poker for it. The winner chooses the destination." We had already taken out the box and the chips from the drawer. Marco burst out laughing and sat at the table, and I took a seat opposite him, serious. I'm almost certain he cheated to make me win. Twenty-four hours later we left for Chile, a trip down memory lane and my experience at age sixteen. Those were unforgettable days spent between meeting up with the people who had been my hosts so many years before and who thought of me as a daughter, and visits to the places I loved the most. I wanted to share with Marco the beauty of those places and in that marvelous country we even managed to forget about ourselves.

Peace. We had found a little serenity in the present time of those wanderings, dazzled by the contrasts of that country, which filled us with wonder at every step. Having climbed to over two thousand meters, we gave ourselves up to the intense colors of the Atacama Desert, the salt pans, the rare pools of water, the pink flamingos in search of food, and the crisp, intensely blue sky. We spent hours holding hands in silence, amazed and overwhelmed by wonder.

I had brightened up. Before me there was only what I could see. Nothing else. Then, one morning there was a sudden change: the pink, the blue, the white of the salt, all faded into infinite shades of gray, the reflection of big clouds that expanded as they raced toward us. A flamingo took flight, leaving its partner alone. A sign.

I was afraid that something might happen to us there, in that place. We went back to San Pedro and the next day we traveled on. My angst disappeared and I felt safe once more, with Marco.

"Let's stay here. I don't want to go back home," I said, more to myself than to him. We were sitting by the side of the swimming pool in the resort where we were staying. My legs were bent, my heels on the edge of the seat, my arms around my knees. I was embracing myself, happy in the present yet deeply troubled.

"You may well be, my princess," Marco joked, "but we can't just drop everything. Besides, would you trade New York for this? Really?" With a broad sweep of his arm he indicated the surroundings.

"If we don't stay, this will be our paradise lost." I sniffed. It was the first time I had wept since we had left. Our brief vacation would end the next day. "If we stay in Chile, we'll run no risks. Nothing can get to us here," I breathed the words out, my eyes glistening, my shaking hands around my kneecaps. "Do you see? Here we are safe." A sob put a stop to my nonsense. Marco didn't move, his head lowered. After a couple of minutes he got up. His posture was that of an old man with many years and sorrows weighing on his hunched shoulders. Without looking at me he said, "Come on, Anna. Let's go do the packing."

*** 

We left for New York on December 30.

The fatigue of the trip hit me as soon as we boarded the plane. During the flight I pretended to snooze so as not to make conversation with Anna. My mind was again full of medical tests, conversations with Dr. Flores, therapy, meetings at the office in which I was on the defensive, on the lookout for any sympathetic looks from my colleagues. I had told none of them about the seriousness of my illness, but my absences, hospital stays and weight loss were not hard to interpret for anyone. I no longer believed the doctors' prognoses.

Then there was Anna. Now she was refusing to talk to me about what was happening; I would have liked to confide in her for as long as I had the breath to get the words out, to explain to her how I was making arrangements so that she would have no problems when I passed. I would leave her the time and a way to get used to my absence, without her having to deal with other worries.

I wanted security for my Anna.

Her memory of me would slowly fade, after much effort and suffering. It would be hard, very hard. I had told her mother that, too. Sveva knew right from the start that I would have no way out, she had realized that even before I did. She was an intelligent woman, and I could trust her.

240

Anna would go through the uninterrupted silence of my presence with her ears stopped up, her face wet with tears, her legs wobbly, and her stomach in knots. Anna! On her solitary journey she would be accompanied by fragments of memory, a taste rediscovered, old photos, music, and videos with our words.

In the end I fell asleep for real and didn't wake up until the landing gear hit the runway at JFK.

"Did you have a good rest?" Anna was smiling, our hands still laced together.

"You let me sleep. Why?" I already regretted having left her alone for so long, she who was afraid of flying.

"I had a nap, too." Now were in line with the others, close to the aircraft steps. Anna tidied her hair with her hands. "I can't wait to have a shower," she mumbled in the middle of a badly suppressed yawn. "By the way, why don't we invite a few friends for tomorrow evening?"

"No. Let's not."

"Why?" she asked with her stormy look, eyes wide open and eyebrows arched. "Surely you don't want us to spend the last day of the year alone?"

"But I do." I didn't say anything else, but she understood I was afraid it might be our last New Year's Eve together. I had no certainty I would survive until the next one.

"No one knows what's going to happen." Anna replied to my unspoken thought. "We might as well celebrate in company and not think about it."

"I don't want to."

"And I don't want us to be alone. I want to do something. Either we invite someone or we go out." She was angry and ready to give battle. There was resentment in her voice. She was frightened.

We retrieved our baggage and headed for the cabstand. As I sat down in the car, I made an odd movement, a kind of twist that gave me a dull ache in my back. I thought it would go after a hot bath.

It never went away.

My days were spent between the hospital and the office; I was spending almost more time in examinations, tests and therapies than I did at work, yet when summer came it seemed as if the illness had granted me a respite. I felt strong enough to face the vacation in Italy. Maybe it was the desire to see my old man and my brother, my friends and my sea, that gave me the illusion of a physical recovery. Anna was excited by the idea of our departure. She zoomed around the house frenetic as a hummingbird while I lay sprawled out on the couch pretending to work on my laptop while I watched her go from one room to another or heard her opening closet doors and shutting drawers. She was murmuring unintelligible stuff, then every now and then she appeared in the living room and dumped an armful of clothes on the cushions next to me.

"What do you say? Shall I take this?" She held up to her bosom the umpteenth magnolia-white dress, one of many in her boundless collection.

"Sure. It's my favorite." I tried to be serious.

"And this? What do you think of this? But I had it last year already. Sofia will definitely remember it."

"Sure. It's my favorite." Now I was grinning as she threw the dress at me.

"You scamp! Don't make fun of me. Give me a hand with the bags, you're making me do everything myself." She was as happy as a little girl in that moment of good humor. Occasionally we forgot about us, about our life now, and went back to the way we used to be. But Anna was thinner than before, she seemed made of tissue paper, whereas I had filled out nicely and I was sure no one at home would have had anything to say about my appearance. The massive doses of cortisone had fleshed out my decline.

Entering the house in Fano brought me back to my mother, but the memory of her became first a presence and then a presentiment. When I went into the kitchen, everything that had been important until a minute before ceased to exist, and in fact I saw her. She was standing in front of the sink doing something, but as soon as she heard me she turned around and held out her hands, smiling.

"Marco, are you well?"

"Dad!" I came out of the vision and hugged my father, finding him old, as I would never be. Before I could give in to my emotions, my brother, Sofia and the children were all over me. Just the time to say hello and they shoved me toward the table laden with my favorite things and in the meantime they vied with one another to compliment me and tell me how well I looked. I alone knew I was an actor with perfect stage makeup.

After dinner, as usual, Anna began distributing the presents we had brought from New York. Each package triggered little cries of joy, endless comments, questions and jubilant exclamations. They were all happy and it was great to see them like that, gathered around her as she handed out chat and little parcels. I would have liked to stay there forever, in that room, in that moment.

"Are you eating here tonight or do you have a date with friends? Did you let them know you were coming? We've told your aunts and uncles." Sofia was tidying up ribbons and boxes, salvaging any useful packaging.

"I don't know. Maybe Marco is tired..." Anna was behind me, massaging my neck. I took her hands and turned around to look at her: "Tonight let's eat here, all together. I want to be with family. There'll be time for friends."

"Good!" Matteo said with an enthusiasm that struck me as a little strained. "That way you can tell me how things are going at work." He was scrutinizing me attentively. Now the initial chaos had passed, he was looking for the signs of illness in my face; maybe all he saw was that I was serene and he was reassured; in fact, his face opened into a smile.

In the afternoon Anna and I went to lie down on the bed. The summer light filtered through the slats of the blinds, lending the room an other-worldly dimension. Anna fell asleep straight away while, despite the tiredness of the journey and the jet lag, I couldn't follow suit. I was happy to be back in Fano. Stretched out on the bed, in the room immersed in a kind of dusty face powder made evident by the rays of sunlight that cut through the shadow, I felt good. I wanted to embrace Anna, hold her close, and tell her it was nothing, a minor setback, and that she didn't have to worry because we two, she and I, were special and everything would work out.

I didn't do that, instead I lay motionless, weeping in silence. I consoled myself and decided I had to begin my farewell. I went around all my friends and listened to their stories and plans, I went to the places where I had had good times, where I had spent my childhood and adolescence, I ate my favorite things without denying myself anything and spent many evening hours sitting on the wall in front of the house, smelling the night and chatting with my brother. Anna and Sofia were sunk deep in the wicker armchairs, exchanging confidences I wouldn't be let in on. Every so often they turned to look at us. Anna nursed me with her eyes.

In the mornings we went to the beach or took a stroll around the streets of the town or maybe we went up to walk in the hills. Anna and I held hands always. One day we were sitting on a bench along the seafront, I had my arm around her and she had her head in the hollow of my shoulder. "We shall always be together," she said seriously. I didn't reply, I silently prayed that it was true, but I didn't believe in God. Not anymore.

I spent a lot of time with the children; we played on the beach and at home in the yard with the hose and the sprinkler. They managed to take my mind off myself, at least for a few hours.

The last day of the vacation, right after lunch, I took Anna and Sofia by the hand and obliged them to go out with me.

"It's too hot. Where do you want to go? My sister-in-law protested.

"Yes, she's right. Let's go and rest, we can go out later." Anna spoke for me.

"I want to buy you a gelato in the square and after that I have a surprise."

Both of them pricked up their ears, but I didn't breathe a word as we ate our enormous sundaes, sitting on the swing seats in the best ice cream parlor in Fano.

"Give us a clue. Come on, Marco!" Sofia pestered me.

"Ignore him, don't give him any satisfaction" Anna added. I didn't reply, but concentrated on my chocolate chip ice cream and enjoyed my moment. When the church bells struck four, I got up and went to pay while, chatting together, they followed.

"Now where are we going?" Anna asked.

"To the other side of the square. Look. Gino is opening now." I pointed to the jewelry store on the corner with the avenue. I gently nudged them forward. Anna was smiling, the crafty thing, while Sofia kept asking what she had to do with any of this. I didn't answer until a few minutes later, at Gino, the jeweler's. "Have the ladies choose what they wish."

"Sure. I'll see to that," he replied.

"The budget?" Anna's eyes glittered—she was making her play.

"What do you fancy, Anna? Come on, I'll help you choose." Sofia was standing shoulder to shoulder with my love.

"No, my dear. Think about yourself. I believe a choker would look good on you," I broke in, signaling to Gino.

"Why? Me?" Now she took a step back, opening her eyes wide. Embarrassment caused a slight blush to creep up her cheeks.

"Here we are, the emerald rings and the necklaces." Gino unrolled several velvet cloths on which gold and precious stones glittered.

"Did we discuss emerald rings?" I asked.

"Yes." Anna was already trying one on. "I never waste time. You know that." She was laughing happily. On the other hand, it was difficult to persuade Sofia to try something on. When she realized that accepting that present was a gift from her to me, and not the other way around, she then tried to make me spend the minimum possible and we argued, in fun, for a while.

In the end, it took my mind off my illness, but then I suddenly remembered it. When memory steps in at the wrong time. I felt a stabbing pain in my back once more, a strong one. I didn't bat an eyelid as I was paying. Before we went out I kissed Anna on the mouth as the others looked on in embarrassment.

It was the last time I gave Anna a gift of jewelry.

# 27
## PANETTONE AND NUTELLA

*New York, September 2013*

Everything had to be as it always had been. As I was setting
the table for breakfast I persuaded myself that if I did everything in the usual way, the day would not have any nasty surprises in store. I had been repeating that to myself every day
in those months, pretending that we weren't sinking into the
quicksand that sooner or later would swallow up what was
left of us.

The house was as it had been during the happy times and
we were Anna and Marco, the ideal couple. That morning the
headache was accompanied by tension, something that happened to me more and more often. I would take something
right away, nothing was to spoil our time together.

I ran a hand over the perfectly ironed white linen tablecloth. I looked at the two white plates, one opposite the other,
the cutlery, the cups, the sugar in a transparent jar and the
Nutella, the basket with three fragrant croissants just bought
from the baker's, and the Bialetti Moka coffee pot, piping hot.

"It's ready. Are you coming?" I whispered the question,
knowing I would get no answer.

Marco was still asleep. Besides, it was Saturday. I had gotten up early, out of habit. I liked to prepare the mixture for

the cake he called the 'panettone.' During the week Marco ate a slice at breakfast, filling it with Nutella and then eating it in little mouthfuls, chewing slowly with a beatific air. For him, Nutella was a staple food, indispensable.

When I put the cake in the oven, I went out to buy the croissants. I enjoyed taking a short morning walk by myself. During the weekend New York changed rhythm only for me. It slowed down. Once the buildings and the windows used to tell me they loved me, that I was lucky, and that Marco and I would have a great future amid the smoke and the concrete. 'You're special,' the city whispered, 'I'll protect you.' I wanted to believe that the promise made by the Big Apple was still good.

Despite everything.

Usually, I stayed out for a half hour, the time the cake took to bake. When I got back, I would almost always find Marco had just got up. Often, he was making coffee or, if he was still asleep, I would wake him with a few cuddles and he would give me the first smile of the day. Now, instead, I had to wait for him to wake up. I was sitting on the couch, running an eye over the Italian newspapers on my iPad, first the *Corriere* and then *la Repubblica*. It was a habit we shared, he and I, looking at America from the inside through the eyes of someone far away. Sometimes the comparison between our reality and the view from Italy was really amusing, but it confirmed the unbridgeable gap between two countries, one stationary and the other rushing onward.

I listened in the direction of the open bedroom door. I could hear Marco's regular breathing and, now and then, the rustling of sheets. He was turning over in bed, trying to rest, to prolong the blissful oblivion of sleep, partly because he needed to recover from the chronic fatigue caused by the therapy, and partly so as not to think.

248

In the meantime, I moved on to other papers, to the *New York Times*; I concentrated on world news—it was one way of getting away from the black cloud that no longer moved from our home.

I respected his sleep, but I was restless, even impatient. I couldn't wait to have Marco with me. I was patient with my love. I had always been so. I liked to care for him, to please him, maybe a legacy of my being Italian and raised in a very traditional provincial family; nonetheless I was chomping at the bit over those hours, minutes, and seconds of life that time spent asleep was stealing from us.

But I waited.

I waited still and always.

An empty bag that hoped to be filled.

By his love.

Sometimes we communicated only by being close, in silence, or through small talk. At times Marco would begin to say things I refused to listen to.

It happened one evening, just after we had gone to bed. Now he was always the first to go to bed and he would wait for me there with eyes shut, lying on his back, neat and tidy. When I slipped between the sheets he reached out his arm and we wound our fingers together. One minute after that his voice came to me.

"Anna." He squeezed my fingers tight.

"Yes, love."

"Today I sorted out all the insurance papers. This week I'll see to the transfer of the policies. They must all be in your name."

"I'm not interested. Rather, at what time is your appointment with the doctor tomorrow?"

"I'll go alone. It's mid-afternoon. You have your own things to see to."

"I'll shift my appointments, it doesn't matter."

"Don't shift anything. It's a routine examination. There won't be anything new. Besides I prefer to go alone. I waste less time. And then you always bring me cakes in our tea room." He gave a little laugh. I was struck by the doubt that, now more than ever, he wanted to manage his illness without me, to filter the news, but I whisked that thought away as I would an annoying fly. He was holding up well, he was still the usual Marco. That's how I saw him. I turned toward him and hugged him. "Okay, if that's what you want."

More and more often he would free himself from my embrace with a sigh, "Come on, let's go to sleep. I'm tired." We would lie awake in the darkness, motionless, for hours.

Almost always he was the first to fall asleep. I noticed the rhythm of his breathing change and grow slower, eventually becoming a gentle snore. I remained a little longer in the grip of the dark and muddled thoughts of the night, the kind you try to repel but draw you into a vortex of dreadful feelings, with anxiety clutching at your throat, my tears running silently down to wet the pillow until, drained, and god knows how, I fell into the oblivion of deep sleep.

The next morning our performance began again as we tried, less successfully with every passing day, to pretend that everything was going well.

In reality we had lost contact with our old life. Marco still kept his smile, but now it had dimmed, I continued to organize little pranks and special moments in which we played at the princess and the knight, but the spell was broken.

"I've transferred my checking account into your name. It's all in order, all you have to do is go and sign." Marco looked satisfied, almost triumphant. I burst into tears.

"Anna, don't do that. I don't want you to have problems. Come on!" He ran his fingers over my wet cheeks.

"Don't say these things." I noticed that my voice had grown shrill, but I couldn't control myself. "There won't be any problems. You'll see to everything."

"Cheer up, Anna." He held me close and I returned his embrace. His body, the body that was my home, was shrinking. Where before there had been curves I now encountered sharp edges; I could feel bone through skin grown thin. Yet not much time had passed since my hands had caressed him and felt the pulse of life, the warmth of desire, and hope for the future. Now I didn't want to accept the possibility that everything that was happening had a definitive significance.

Marco was leaving me.

Every so often I would think about it, when I was alone. I imagined myself standing in a corner of the living room, by the window. Our home empty with no more Marco and not even a piece of furniture, nothing that marked our belonging to that place. Not even our smell. Outside, much lower down, New York pulsated like a big beating heart. No, it was a ravenous beast, a predator. Waiting for me.

Alone in the naked house, I sensed the noise filtered by the windows; I remembered, since I knew it well, the stink of gas, rubber and street food, mixed with smoke and sweat and the human presence I was accustomed to and loved.

Suddenly I couldn't breathe. The survival instinct brought me back to the present. I usually found myself soaked in sweat, my face wet with unrestrained tears, and my stomach on fire.

I hated the end, our end.

To keep it at bay, I withdrew to my limbo, convincing myself that they were horrible fantasies. I used thousands of stratagems to avoid the reality of our destinies. I would have liked more time to devote to my love, but I used work as a free zone and never said no to any client.

I wanted to be with him and at the same time I wanted to be far from him. I wanted our life from before that I could no longer have. I wanted a series of normal days, without that constant, heart-rending pain that grew a little every day. There was no room for anything else, yet I pretended—we pretended—to be among those who have a life before them.

The empty refrigerator and the shopping no longer counted for anything, we no longer attended condo board meetings nor did we stop to chat with neighbors; we avoided all encounters and furtively peered outside the door before leaving to make sure no one was in the corridor. I still went to the hairdresser's because being well groomed was a duty, but I didn't recognize myself in the mirror.

I no longer knew who I was because I had lost my future.

I wept more and more often. The tears came unexpectedly, with no control.

I remember one afternoon, it was late—almost dinnertime—and instead of going home, I had to drop by the office. I had spent the entire day crossing New York from the Upper West Side to Tribeca via the Lower East Side, always in a rush to hop from one appointment to the next, and everything had gone wrong.

Marco was at home. I imagined him sitting on the little wicker armchair as he worked at the computer, checking his watch from time to time. He was waiting patiently. The tears began to flow and when the sliding doors opened at my floor I was sobbing. I went along the corridor and arrived at the office door sniffing. I thought I was alone, but the cleaning lady was there: a fat, slow woman .

I stopped dead and she looked at me in surprise. "What's the matter, ma'am?" She had an almost maternal air and I started crying again even louder.

"You're tired, aren't you? You people here work too much. Go home." She glanced at my hands. "Go to your husband. It's not worth crying over work. Everything will be okay, you'll see. Tomorrow will be better."

I looked at her and said nothing, but I stopped crying. The job made my life difficult, but sometimes it took me away from my torment for a few hours. Nonetheless, the guilty feelings for the time I was taking away from Marco were unbearable. I, working in a young and healthy body. I, destined to remain while he wasted away.

Yet in the course of our last summer, that of 2013, I took on any job, even those that kept me away from home on Saturdays, Sundays, and evenings, too. I didn't like to leave Marco alone even though he encouraged me not to miss any opportunity and showed that he was glad for me.

Oppressed by guilt feelings, I would get ready, kiss him and leave, wanting to stay as I hurried toward the elevator and then toward the subway. I was in the middle of the crowds where everything seemed normal. I negotiated with clients, explained, joked and pretended to be cheerful while my thoughts were filled with a vision of Marco without me. Sometimes I ran back home, risking an ankle injury because of the high heels. I couldn't wait to hold him close in my arms, but there were days when I didn't want to admit even to myself that I wanted to run away.

That was the time I cried the most; I felt guilty, troubled by the commission of my sin—I wished to flee from all this suffering. Sometimes I sobbed, sweated, trembled, and I could smell the odor of my betrayal on my skin. Instead, Marco consoled me, congratulated me on my successes and then, in quiet moments, when we were alone in a semblance of peace, he would start saying strange things again, "It doesn't matter if it's late. What matters is that you closed a deal. You're pleased with yourself. I'm glad." He was smiling as I put together an improvised pasta dish, then he sat on the stool and watched me set the table. By that time every little thing made him tired, yet I pretended not to notice so as not to humiliate him.

"Anna, afterward I'm going to show you where we keep the list of passwords. I've reorganized it, dividing it up into categories and putting it in alphabetical order and..."

"What's got into you? I'm not interested, anyway, you've always looked after the passwords."

"It may be your turn to do that, you know. You'll need to know how to get into the bank." He managed to say this with a sly smile—he seemed even happy. It broke my heart. "You're hurting me, do you see that? I don't want your damned list. I'm not interested." I raised my voice, angry on the outside and dejected inside.

I didn't admit it, but there was no way out. I finished setting the table, slamming down the plates with my head bent and my hair hanging down over my drawn face, so as not to show the tears. In those moments, when he threw reality in my face and brought me abruptly back to Earth, leaving me no escape, I felt like slapping him.

It ended with us eating in silence. He tried to be funny a few times, but I held my ground and then, after I had straightened up the kitchen, I curled up on the couch beside him like a cat, seeking contact with the body that no longer looked like him.

My disquiet grew with every passing day. In the mornings I went out without eye makeup. I already knew that the first tears would come as soon as I set foot in the street. I wept in the subway, the office, locked in the bathroom, and sobbed once more when I was home alone.

'What am I doing?' I thought. 'I should be spending all my time with Marco and instead...' Instead, I was refusing to accept what I had already known for some time. 'I must stay with him, we must continue to talk as long as possible, as long as we can find the words. It's late, it's late for anything.' Desperation made me lose both sleep and appetite. For some time we had been avoiding mirrors, but one day we happened to catch our reflections in a shop window. We realized that our silhouettes were beginning to look alike: slight, with backs slightly bowed from suffering.

"Anna, you're too thin. How many pounds have you lost?" he asked me in a reproachful tone. I just shook my head and strode away rapidly, bumping into people, careless of the knocks, devastated by what I had glimpsed in the shape of our profiles. I eventually slowed down and when Marco caught up we didn't bring the subject up again.

# 28
# La Vie En Rose

*New York, November 13, 2013*
"Wait up, Anna." Jim caught me by surprise as I was pushing the glass door of 30 Irving Place.

"I'm not running away."

Jim was a big awkward sort of guy. My mother would have called him *un mandolin*—she could describe anyone with a couple of words in her dialect. It wasn't yet eight o'clock and now the elevator doors in front of Jim and me were opening to take us to the ninth-floor offices of the real estate company we worked for.

"I've a proposition to make you," he said with a sly smile. "I've got two tickets for the Maria Bethania concert this evening. Do you know her?"

"No."

"She's this great Brazilian singer. She'll be doing Edith Piaf's most famous songs," he said in triumphal tones.

"Lucky you. I adore Piaf."

"I know and I also know that tomorrow's your birthday. Listen, I can't make it. To tell the truth I'm not interested anymore."

"So you've finally met your match? Have you finally found someone who's stood you up?" I often used to tell Marco about Jim's love life. He was the kind who fell in love at the drop of a hat and changed girlfriends between cocktails and dinner.

"You're wrong. I have better plans and besides, I'd like to make you a present of the tickets. If you go with Marco..."

"A present? They must have been expensive."

"Here they are." He took the tickets from his pocket just as the doors were opening and handed them to me. He gave me a bigger hug than he should have. "Happy birthday, Anna. Good luck with everything." He turned on his heel and took the left-hand corridor.

I took the opposite one, went to my office and called Marco right away.

*** 

I didn't have the heart to say no to Anna. We went to the Maria Bethania concert.

At the office there had been a meeting that went on for longer than expected. At a certain point Rosario had given me a long look. "Go home, Marco. Anyway, we're almost done." But I stayed on until the end.

Work was more important than the concert. Even more than the backache that wouldn't give me a break.

I didn't want to go and, to tell the truth, I didn't think I could stand a couple hours stuck in a not-so-comfortable seat. The pain gave me no respite and I had been on the go since the morning. I checked my calls. Anna was waiting for me, she was already at the theater, so I took a cab to Broadway. I saw her immediately, just outside the entrance. Excited, she came toward me saying that Maria Bethania had only just arrived and the show would begin a little late.

It was fate that we should be late, too. We joined the river of people going to take their seats. Finally I lowered myself carefully into a red seat with Anna beside me. The singer had just appeared on stage, everyone was applauding and I was looking at Anna, her profile, her slightly reddened eyes now trained on Maria Bethania, her thin, almost stylized hands beating against one another in the air.

Perhaps she had been crying. I knew that she wept in secret, in the presence of anyone she didn't know. On the street, in cabs, on the subway. Far from the reach of friends and acquaintances and, especially, far from me.

When Maria Bethania began to sing *La vie en rose*, Anna turned to look at me. She emanated a happiness beyond the memories of what she was living through. She laced her warm hand into my cold sweaty one and gripped it tight. A minute later she kissed me on the cheek.

Kissing me had always come naturally to her, even in the most unexpected moments, regardless of whether we were alone or in the company of friends or a crowd of strangers.

She would take my face in her hands and press my ears, squeezing my lobes between two fingers and then the kiss would come. It might be a light, quick flutter or a real kiss, a loving kiss as I called it, while she said it was a grownup's kiss. The act always shaded into a caress.

Anna was never rough—everything she did was done with grace. She was graceful in spirit, in the way she pleased me to show her love. She wove a tapestry with me in the middle.

I wouldn't have bet two cents on my chances of holding out, stuck in that red seat until the end of the show. In that moment this was my private hell. The wrenching, stabbing pain in my back, amid the general soreness that had been chronic for weeks, was made even more painful by the enforced position.

I was alone, in the auditorium, among hundreds of people having fun and smiling as they watched the stage.

Anna, too, beside me. She squeezed my hand.

I noticed that despite the ravished air with which she followed the show, two shining teardrops had formed on the edges of her eyelashes.

***

I knew Marco wasn't well. I also knew that, despite the pain, he was glad he had come to the theater to make me happy.

But I couldn't ignore his suffering, the unnatural way he was sitting, the little movements to adjust the position of his aching body on the red plush, the breath held for a stab of pain, the mouth open in search of more air, the grimace that forced itself to look like a smile.

Generous.

Loving.

Our time together was the most precious thing, we knew that.

But I felt at fault. I had already sensed he was troubled over the phone, then there had been the delay owing to the prolonged meeting at the office.

"Anna, I'm not sure I can make it." His voice had come to me, feeble, muffled.

"Don't worry. If you can't make it, it doesn't matter."

I tried to hold back my disappointment, not very successfully. But I hadn't said 'some another time.' I didn't admit it, but I knew that time was running out. I pretended there would be at least one more tomorrow.

When I got to the theater, I saw him, handsome as always. He smiled at me and I hugged him desperately. I sniffed at him to hold onto his smell.

'There's time,' I thought. I measured time by a new, fuzzy measure, no longer in months, weeks, days, hours, or minutes. Time was only time. Something that didn't stay within any sure parameter.

There was the time of the thermometer to check his temperature, the cooking time of number five spaghetti, al dente or well cooked, the time of a wash cycle, the time of a song. The time of therapy and that of a smile. The time of a Skype connection with Italy and the time in which I waited for the elevator to arrive and take me up, home, to Marco and my sorrow.

The time of the end.

Time was running out, but the next day was my birthday and everything would go well.

Marco had organized a party with our closest friends. We had prepared for it carefully. I helped him into his good suit, I tightened up the belt around the loose-fitting pants—god how loose they were—and I put on his jacket. What a snappy dresser!

I was looking good, too, and I felt beautiful as I opened the packages and thanked everyone and he cracked jokes and made fun of me. Occasionally he would touch my shoulder or caress my hair, and I took his hand before extricating my fingers to take a new gift and he would brush against me with his voice, with the edge of his jacket, or a casual elbow.

Everything was good as long as contact was maintained.

As I was bringing in the cake, amid the hubbub and the buzz of the guests, Marco had enfolded me in his arms to whisper a few words in my ear: Happy birthday, love! Thirty, a good number. You know that I'm truly happy with you."

His eyes were glistening and so were mine. I went through the ritual of making a wish with eyes closed, my hands behind my back interlaced with his. I blew out the candles. No one dared ask me the usual stupid question about what I had wished for, and anyway, you should never tell.

For luck.

Propitiatory rituals are a fraud. All of them.

By the end of the party Marco was exhausted and it showed. Actually, the party ended because it was clear to everyone that Marco was exhausted. After saying goodbye to the last guests, he went straight to bed.

Now it was night and I was hanging about in the bathroom, examining myself in front of the mirror. 'What a face! Scratch the surface and beneath the makeup you're a fright.'

I thought briefly about me, alone, and then about the baby. I caressed my belly, as I had been doing for a while. A flat, useless stomach. How I would have wanted a child with Marco now.

We had returned to the subject a few evenings before my party. But he had been adamant, "Children are blameless and must not suffer. Try to understand, Anna. I'm asking you to be generous with our child. It's wrong to raise him without a father."

"You are here. You will be here."

"You know that we're about to be separated." With a tired gesture he took my chin to force me to look at him. "You know. Making a baby in the knowledge that he'll never know his father is wrong."

I burst into heart-rending sobs, I was sorry for myself, for Marco and our child who would never be. I was desperate for all of us and Marco consoled me. In bed, locked in an embrace, alone in the world. Defeated between sheets that felt icy to me, as if they had been swept by a stiff breeze that had chilled them.

"Now...before long you'll be able to make another choice, if ever you thought to use my frozen sperm." Marco had been implacable. "I will no longer have room to maneuver to prevent you doing that, but Anna..." He was breathless. He stopped and then began again. "I'm almost certain that you'll respect my wishes and by doing that you'll choose the best path for you, too. And for our child."

On remembering his words I gave a sob.

I put my ear to the door, then I half opened it. Quietly.

Nothing, I could hear nothing.

I moved in the darkness, aided by the blade of light reflected through the blackout drapes. New York was still living in the fast line, outside there.

He was sleeping, his breathing short and light.

Sitting on the bed, I took off my wedding ring and, like every evening, I dropped it into the white leather trinket tray on the bedside table. It hit the rim of the container and bounced off the wooden floor. I turned around straight away to see if the sound had wakened him. Luckily, he slept on.

I stared at the floor once more.

No trace of my wedding ring. I looked around, running my hands over the floor.

It had vanished.

Lying on the floor I inspected the space under the bed. I stretched out an arm to sweep the parquet, but found nothing. Yet the ring had to be there somewhere. I didn't want to risk waking Marco.

I slipped under the covers. I kept feeling my finger where there was a slight indentation left by the ring I had just taken off. I examined the hollow uneasily, the way I used to poke my tongue into the space left by a baby tooth that had just dropped out when I was small.

'Will I wear my ring, afterward?' I immediately regretted the ugly thought.

The morning after my birthday party we woke early. Marco had an appointment with Dr. Flores. He had told me they had to review the therapy situation. After an unenthusiastic breakfast of tea and cookies, Marco sank onto the couch, still tired after his late night. Partying had worn him out and, as usual, he had slept little and badly. For how long had he been unable to sleep? Weeks? Months? I certainly didn't know.

"What time is your examination?"

"It doesn't matter. You go to work. Aren't you running late?"

"Surprise!" I exclaimed bitterly. "I've only one appointment in an hour's time, then I've kept the day free to be with you."

He gave me a sidelong look. "I have to be there at eleven. Can you make that?"

"Sure, love." I put on my jacket, took my handbag and bent down to kiss him, a quick peck on the cheek, and then pretended to tweak the tip of his nose with two fingers. A little private joke that he loved a lot. I wanted to make amends for everything, for something, for nothing.

There was no more room, desire, or idea for anything else. He took my hand and I remained bent over him as he whispered, "Anna, perhaps they're going to take me off the trial."

"Don't even think that. Why would they do something like that? It wouldn't make any sense." The reassuring tone didn't come off well. I pretty much dashed out and grabbed the first cab I saw. At the office I closed the door, canceled the appointment, and called Dr. Flores. I paced up and down the room, between the desk and the window. I felt like a fury, full of energy, ready to give battle.

"Yes, I know. Marco has an appointment with you at 11, right?"

"At 10:30, to be exact" she replied.

"Oh, I see." A half-hour difference that Marco had kept to himself. He had lied to me and goodness knows how many other times he'd done that. "You two are hiding things from me." I thumped the desk with my fist so hard that the sound even reached the doctor.

"Anna, what are you doing? Calm down. You know the situation..."

"I only know what Marco wants to let me know. He has put me aside. I've understood this for a long time."

"Marco isn't hiding anything from you. The last time all three of us met...Only ten days have gone by. I recall that he himself gave you a report on the situation, the therapies."

"I'm not stupid. You two had an agreement. You meet shortly beforehand, you tell him how things really are and when I get there you filter them. I'm not stupid. Do you think I'm stupid?"

"You live with Marco, and you have him by your side every day. At this point I don't have to tell you anything."

"I need to know. What haven't you told me? What? I have to work, I'm out for hours and hours. I must decide..."

"Don't decide, give in." The doctor interrupted me. "Come at eleven o'clock, as Marco said. Indulge him. Now you know all there is to know." She hung up and I slumped into my chair.

Yes, I knew everything and I had lost all my illusions a while back.

For some time, every day I had been watching Marco die. I had spent over a year watching his body waste away month by month, week by week and day by day. Now changes occurred in the space of a few hours. The pain never left him.

The last time we had made love I had measured his bony body against mine. I hadn't recognized it and maybe he had noticed that. Either for that reason or because of the pain, he hadn't sought me anymore. There were other things in play, we knew that, but I had no room for the truth and ignored his hunched posture, his smile that often became a grimace, and his clothes that had become at least two sizes too big. Once he had worn them with elegance and now they hung on him as if draped over a coat hanger.

I hated, refused, and rejected or dismissed the idea of losing him. Yet I knew that I would survive, even though the idea of Anna alone was unbearable.

# 29
## THREE STEPS

*New York, November 15, 2013*
It was all over, I knew it. I had waited for Anna's birthday, to make her happy. Now I couldn't hold things together any longer. The time had come for a change, of course. What would I do about Anna? I was deeply saddened for the sorrow she would feel and because I wouldn't be there to console her. I had fallen into a crevasse. I had fallen into it from the side of life and I knew that on the opposite side there was something I didn't know but would soon encounter.

I was tired, but I decided to take the subway, to be among people. It comforted me to join the stream of people crossing New York for a thousand and one reasons. I was headed Uptown; I changed from line seven to line six and got off at 68th Street, then walked slowly along the road toward the hospital. I thought of the many times Anna and I had taken the same route to the Sloan Kettering. Over the last year and a half, after every examination, my hopes of making it dwindled.

Breathing hurt. Climbing the three steps up to the door was as tiring as swimming across the bay. After endless corridors and the elevator, I arrived at my destination.

"Good morning, Marco, ten-thirty on the dot." Barbara— Dr. Flores— with her dark complexion, a white lab coat and the black pants and the red shoes she liked so much, wore a serious smile. 'My doctor is fond of me,' I thought. "But now comes the reckoning.'

"Are you taking me off the trial program?" I asked, getting straight to the point.

"It's more like a change of trial. We'll discuss it now, I'll explain..." she replied, inviting me to take a seat. She sat on the edge of the desk, facing me.

"It doesn't matter. I get it. So this is it." My voice was shaking. "How much... When?"

"No one can tell for sure. Do as I've always told you: don't think about how much time you have, but try to live your life as you want to. Take time for other things, Marco. Live your hours."

So according to the doctor it was a matter of hours. Hours, not days. I was stunned. "Anna will be here soon. What shall we tell her?"

"Don't worry. I'll see to it. We've another quarter hour before eleven. Is there anything you wish to ask me?"

"I want to tell you about Anna." I sank back against my chair and closed my eyes. "About what she did to celebrate our first wedding anniversary. She asked me to take a day off and made a date to meet me in Bryant Park, our special place. She told me I had to wear my wedding tuxedo. I went there and then she arrived. She was in her wedding dress and she was even more beautiful than she had been the year before. This time the bouquet was of sunflowers. Anna always lives in the sunshine, she can't live in a gloomy climate. She had organized everything, called in a photographer friend. We have a whole album devoted to our first anniversary. We laughed like crazy that day and for many days after. God, how we laughed together. We used to laugh a lot, before." We sat in silence for a while, then I resumed, "That evening, at home, Anna told me that she had wanted to relive our fairy tale wedding. And so she made it live again for me, too. At a certain point she looked at me, such an intense look that for a moment her eyes seemed almost black. The light, I thought. Then she said, 'You know, I'm convinced that if I hadn't made you this surprise for our first anniversary, I wouldn't be able to do it ever again'. Now the doctor was listening to my weeping, in silence. "Anna is the love of my life. I believe I'll carry on loving her from...wherever."

We both heard hurried footsteps, the end of a run. Anna had arrived. She came right into the office without knocking.

"How are you?" She caressed my cheek. "Well, doctor, how shall we proceed?"

"I was telling Marco that there's a chance of new therapies in two centers: Chicago and Boston. They're both on the cutting edge. They've been having success with two experimental solutions precisely for..."

"See, Marco! The doctor is right, we mustn't give up. Boston is better, it's easier to get to. I'll take a leave of absence from work." She couldn't stop talking, her tone was feverish. Poor Anna. She'd been flung into an unhappiness she didn't deserve. But who deserves any kind of unhappiness? It's part of life and I was almost resigned to mine, which was ending. Every now and then I had had a resurgence of foolish hope, but I had already played my cards and this time lady luck had turned her back on me.

And on Anna too, for now, but in her case the wind might change again later on.

When we took our leave of the doctor, Barbara squeezed my hands for a long time. I knew it was a definitive farewell even though I didn't want to believe it.

Anna and I found ourselves alone, on the street, in the midst of people who couldn't imagine what was happening to us.

"Do you feel up to walking a little? Anna asked. I said yes, to make her happy. It might be our last walk together.

It lasted ten yards. "Wait, get a cab. I'm too tired." Anna turned her pretty face up to me, her eyes full of tears. She hugged me tight and I felt her shiver.

"Do you mind going by yourself in the cab? There's something I have to do for work. It won't take long."

I pretended to believe her excuse and took the ride alone; I was afraid of the pain and the fear she felt for me.

Outside the window, the skyscrapers, the city's menhirs, faded into a low, sullen sky. The uninterrupted coming and going of vehicles and people, which I had always liked so much, was now moving like a broken needle on a vinyl record. All was as before, yet everything had changed because I saw things with different eyes.

Meanwhile, we had arrived. The driver waited for me to get out of the car. I stuck one leg out and then the other, with an effort, as I tried to get my breath and gather the strength necessary get on my feet.

"Come on, buddy. I'll help you." I hadn't even noticed that the driver, a bearded black guy, was at my side, ready to help me. I grabbed his hand and got to my feet on the edge of the sidewalk. "Thanks," I said.

"Woulda took us till sundown otherwise," he replied as he got back into the driver's seat. The car slid into the traffic like an alligator into the swamp.

# 30
## BLUE

*New York, November 15, 2013*
I had expected too much. He was exhausted, I could see that perfectly well, yet I had asked him to walk. That had been cruel on my part.

I will never forget that embrace in the middle of the street, in front of the hospital. I was clinging to him, my ear against his shoulder, listening to his breathing. It sounded different than usual: short, shallow, gurgling.

It was a mere memory of breath, a remnant that struggled to make way. I was seized by a terrible numbness and hugged Marco for a long time. I was sure that if I let him go I would lose my balance and fall down.

We were two human wrecks, one clinging to the other, amid the chaos of New York, locked up in our grief, prisoners in the leaden gray atmosphere, cloaked in gusts of icy wind, while passersby brushed past without even noticing us.

Alone with no way out. Alone even with ourselves.

Perhaps I would be even more alone before long.

All of a sudden the city was my friend no longer.

I hailed a cab and helped Marco into the car. It was a slow, laborious operation.

"Go home, I'll join you later. I must...Can you make it?" I smiled at him, dying with shame. "I'll take the subway, I'll be quick." He nodded and waved at the driver to move off. He was exhausted.

I wanted to be alone. At least for a while.

I couldn't take the pressure anymore, I couldn't hold out any longer. When I got to the subway station, I hung around there for a little while, to waste time. I parted the carpet of fallen leaves with the toe of my shoe, then I took one step after another, taking care to slide the soles along the blacktop. I walked like that for a few dozen yards, as far as the intersection. I turned back, spent. I was at the subway once more.

Maybe it would do me good to walk for another block. With the taste of the morning's tea and biscuits in my mouth and my stomach in knots, I didn't feel good. I felt ugly, too. Desperation and distress make you horrible. I had to get through all this, I was in deep. 'Swim, Anna,' I told myself.

I took the subway home. Now I wanted to get there fast, at the same time as Marco's taxi, even though being in the house with him scared me.

I didn't want to go home and I wanted to be there already.

It wasn't right that I was alone in this situation.

The sorrow, the sorrow, the sorrow.

I was cold, the wind had strengthened and everything was gray. I ran from the subway to our door.

Marco was in the living room, sitting at the table in the wicker armchair, with the scarf that had been his companion for some months wrapped twice around his neck. The computer in front of him was on.

"Do you feel better? What are you doing?" I asked, caressing his hair.

"I'm almost done checking a report. There's something not right. I'm going to call Rosario."

"Do you really *have* to work? Come on, sit on the couch with me." I had taken the iPad to have a look at the news, to take my mind off things. To be close to him but far from there, at least in my mind.

"No, I'll call him. I'll be quick. But my stomach hurts, I feel queasy."

"Have you caught a cold?" I got up to feel his brow, and it was cool. "Maybe you've eaten something that disagreed with you. I'll fix you a chamomile tea or a tisane." He was already speaking over the phone, and anxiety welled up in my throat. Marco had never suffered from nausea since I'd known him. I stayed in the kitchen, waiting for the kettle to boil. When it whistled I had the tray ready with the cup, the tea bag and the sugar. I poured in the boiling water and took the tray into the living room.

"Oh, Anna, come here. Your mom's on Skype. Say hello to her." Marco got up and went to sit on the couch and I put the tray down on the coffee table in front of him. As I did all these simple things, I counted my steps. I didn't think about anything. Only the steps it took to go from the kitchen to the couch and then from the couch to the table. I got rid of my mother quickly. She must have guessed something was up, but her expression on the monitor transmitted even more distress to me. I had no need to add to the burden.

I went back to Marco and snuggled down beside him. He was drinking the chamomile very slowly, blowing on the vapor between one sip and the next. Now his eyes were glistening, but not with tears. They looked strange, undecipherable.

I touched his brow again and, irritated, he pushed my hand away.

"How do you feel? Is it getting better?"

"I don't know." He put down the cup still half full. "That's enough," he said. He massaged his stomach and belly with a slow, circular movement. He tried to take deep breaths but struggled to do so, making a sound that worried me even more.

A wheeze. It was the same sound I had heard him make a few hours before when I hugged him. Now it had crept out of his body, filling the room and resounding in my ears.

And still I didn't understand.

It was the moment. Now? That moment?

No. I was certain it wasn't.

An ailment, a new trouble added to the others, certainly there was still time.

I wouldn't even think that word, I couldn't say it, especially if associated with him. With my love. I rubbed his back lightly.

We didn't have the courage to say anything. We couldn't speak. Minutes went by. Marco was soaked in sweat.

"I'm going to get a cloth." I was already on my feet and he reached out a hand to hold mine. "Wait. Maybe I'm going to vomit." Now his color was verging on green. He seemed changed, the skin of his face too taut, his pupils dilated. He was eaten away from the inside.

I helped him get up and led him to the bathroom. He was struggling to move, I was struggling to hold him up. The pair of us staggering along like some strange human giraffe.

"Come on, darling. Here we are, Easy. This way." Eventually we made it to the bathroom, in front of the toilet bowl.

Marco said nothing, and his eyes were glassy. He gave a kind of hiccup and then vomited blood, dark and dense blood, a lot of blood. His legs buckled and I gently accompanied his fall. I don't know where I got the strength from. The blood spread out over the sky-blue tiles of our bathroom, decorated with the colors of Provence. A memory flashed across my mind: the sun and the colors of our honeymoon.

Something was happening that we weren't prepared for. I helped him lie down on the floor, on his side, to prevent him from suffocating. The odor that saturated the room, like rusty iron, filled my nostrils.

"Marco, I'll get help." I went to get our best pillow. Marco had given it to me during a trip to Miami, on it was written 'Kiss me goodnight.' I slipped the pillow under his head to make him comfortable while I tried to dial 911. The cellphone showed no signal. Why?

"Anna, I'm afraid. I don't understand..." More blood, a lot of it. His eyes were a bottomless pit. I didn't know what to do.

"Try to remain calm. I'm going to call now. They know what to do."

"The blood, here..." He moved his arm in a slow, hesitant gesture, and his voice was a whisper. "All dirty. Look what a mess I've made." He even tried for a smile.

"It doesn't matter, darling. Now I'm going away for a moment. To ask for help. Are you comfortable? Are you cold?" I left him without waiting for an answer. I went out onto the landing and rang the neighbors' doorbell. Luckily Jeff and Linda were home. Linda called 911.

\*\*\*

Lying on my side, my head on the pillow, I waited for Anna. She was usually punctual. But *this time* there was a problem. Anna and I were separated. Separated? No, maybe that wasn't it. We were no longer close like before. The thing that had happened...Impossible to turn back. She has always been brave. She'll hold out.

Yet I could still feel her hand, tender, warm, and damp, caressing my own. I had to let her go; outside the sky was brightening, no more clouds for me.

I was going, it was time, I had to find a way to finish, but Anna still kept me here. I had to be sure she learned to consummate her grief, get used to solitude, and manage to console herself.

\*\*\*

I had gone straight back to Marco. Now his gaze was distant. All he said was, "Anna, call my brother." I began to weep and said his name over and over in between sobs. He didn't respond. His breathing, through his open mouth, was irregular, discontinuous. He was trying to draw air from his stomach. I could see that.

His features were distorted by the effort. In that moment he was alone in his struggle, all alone. Still alive.

He gave me no more words.

Mechanically I made the call to Matteo. This time the cell phone did its duty. What would I say to him? I would pass him to Marco of course. Better that way.

I heard voices—it was the paramedics. They asked me some questions about Marco's condition. There wasn't much space in the bathroom and they asked me to leave, telling Linda to take me to her house. I wasn't to get in their way. Of course, it was right. I understood. I left.

It seemed an unreal scene. That woman wasn't me and the man lying on the bloodstained floor wasn't Marco. It wasn't happening to us. I was already at the door when I turned back.

"Help him, please. He has cancer. Please!" In the meantime, the cell phone display had lit up, the line with Italy was open. Matteo was on the other end. Now there were too many people in our house: Jeff pushed me toward Linda, telling her to take me to their apartment next door straight away. The confusion was terrific. I was speaking with Matteo, telling him that Marco was sick, very sick indeed. Perhaps the tone of my voice was too high, I wasn't controlling myself.

I recall that after a few minutes a doctor came to me, saying there was no pulse and asking me if I wanted them to try to resuscitate him.

RESUSCITATE HIM!

"Of course. He's young. Have you seen how young he is? He has cancer. Resuscitate him, I beg you." Jeff and Linda took me by the arm to take me away. I clawed at the back of the couch. "He's only thirty-three. I beg you!" I screamed, trying to free myself from my friends' grip. I had to stay close to Marco, he needed me.

After a few minutes the paramedics came back, all together. I remember I was standing in the middle of the living room and I backed into the corner by the window. Without crying or saying anything anymore.

'My back's to the wall,' I thought. 'It's finished.' In that moment, miraculously, my eyes were dry but I felt that inside me blocks of ice were breaking away; I felt them slide against my breastbone and ribs, where they melted away into nothingness.

One of the paramedics reached out a hand and gave my shoulder a squeeze. They were good looking young men, strong, healthy, with open faces and apologetic expressions.

"It's all over. We're sorry, but he's gone."

Unacceptable. I didn't reply.

"Ma'am? Did you understand? Sadly, he's dead. Do you understand what we're saying?"

I understood, but I couldn't accept it.

I ran into the bathroom and lay down beside Marco, who was covered by a white sheet. I caressed his face and wove my hand into his through the cloth.

I would have liked to stay there forever, with my love. I held my breath, because he was breathing no more, yet I still lived.

It was over, over forever.

Death had come.

I didn't have to hold back my tears anymore, nor could I have done. I don't know for how long I laid beside him, the man I could no longer see. I kissed him through the sheet.

A very short time had passed since he and I had been talking on the couch. His shape was still impressed on the cushions, the echo of his voice still resounded in the air, and I had his smell on me. God, the smell of blood.

Marco, my Marco, he was all that I had. Now he was here, covered by a sheet, motionless. I felt I had a pain in my stomach, too.

Someone was talking near me, then there was a sudden brief silence until eventually one of the paramedics lifted me up bodily, at least so it seemed. He asked me several times if I had understood what had happened. Yes, I had understood that Marco had gone and that our life was over.

"Now you're going over there, to your friends' house. We have things to do here. To prepare. Then we'll call you." Somehow or other they got me to the door, which was already open. Linda enfolded me in a hug. Jeff put the cell phone in my hand as he had me sit down at the table in his living room. "Your brother-in-law is on the phone," he told me. "I've explained to him. Is there anything you want to say to him?"

"Hello…" Matteo's voice came from far away. I wasn't listening. He said, "I want to bring him back home. He must stay here, by the sea, in his place. Will you help me?" I handed the phone back to Jeff, who ended the call. I didn't know where to stay, or rather, I wanted to stay with Marco. I got up to go toward the door and Linda brought me back to my chair. "Wait. They'll tell us when we can go back there."

I called my mother—she didn't seem surprised, only deeply saddened. It had been hard for me to tell her that Marco had gone. I didn't know how to say it; he was still there, separated from me only by a wall, a few steps, but beyond reach.

Eventually the door of our house—Anna and Marco's house—was opened. The paramedic from before told me I could say my last goodbye to Marco. Jeff went in before me. "Better not lift up the sheet yet, Anna. You'll see him later, when they've cleaned him up." I obeyed.

Once more I felt the outline of his half-open lips through the sheet. I gave him a last kiss. I ran my fingertips over his features and then they told me it was time. They were taking him away. I nodded. Impossible that he should leave that way, yet it was happening. They put Marco—Marco's body, him—in a large blue bag. He had always liked blue. His drawers were full of shirts in various shades of blue: light blue, sea blue, electric blue, cornflower blue, blue…I accompanied him to the elevator.

The doors closed with a crash. Strange, normally they made a wheezing puff, like a bellows.

I put my ear to the metal to listen to the sound of the pulleys moving as he went down.

Jeff and Linda made me go back to their house. I wasn't to stay on my own. I dashed to the window; I wanted to see Marco going away. Outside, New York glittered in the darkness. I tried to follow the gleaming of the cars reflected in the store windows, the colored signs over bars and restaurants, pink, green, blue.

Blue.

It was the beginning of my *after*.

# 31
## DEATH IS TIDY

Devastated, I was on the verge of drowning in desperation, but I wasn't alone for long. As soon as they heard of Marco's death, Matteo and my mother flew over from Italy; the cousins from Connecticut also arrived as well as friends from all over.

Marco had been placed in a large room, in an orderly building on a straight road where the houses were perfectly aligned. In front of the entrance there was a box hedge that also lined the driveway; it was so well manicured that it looked fake. I couldn't say in which neighborhood it was, because I wasn't allowed to go there by myself. I had demanded that I see to everything my love needed. I chose his best clothes for him: a very elegant gray suit with matching vest and a white shirt.

After much thought I decided I wouldn't oblige him to wear a tie, which he had always detested. For the shoes, I had him wear comfortable slip-ons. He would have to travel a long road, without me.

He was beautiful.

Lying in satin.

I kept him company willingly. Only on the last day, that of the funeral, did we not meet. My mother told me he had changed, that it was better I didn't see him and that besides, I had already bidden him farewell. I trusted her words. I sent Marco a kiss, from afar.

There was a big crowd at the service. The Valentino offices were deserted for the duration of the funeral.

Then everyone returned to their own lives and their usual occupations. It wasn't easy, but I persuaded Matteo and my mother to go back home. Once I got through the paperwork I would take Marco back to Italy and I wanted to do it by myself.

Sunk in the seat on the Boeing 767, taking off from JFK New York, I felt confused, leaden. Too many thoughts in my head that weighed me down and none that might take me in any precise direction. I was at a crossroads and I was lost for the first time in my life. I would find my way again, I knew, but there was a hard time to get through first. I needed a respite.

I glanced at my traveling companions. I hadn't exchanged as much as a hello with any of them. Some were reading, some sleeping, others trying to shake off drowsiness. All I wanted was to sink into a state of insensibility, but the lorazepam was less effective than usual. 'Please let me sleep,' I prayed to myself. 'I just want to sleep,' I felt sleep coming, finally. It came with a rancid taste in my mouth. The last image before falling asleep was that of the coffin being swallowed up in the belly of the airplane.

Upon our arrival, Matteo and Sofia took care of everything. We found a way to keep the secret from Marco's father, who was too old and too sick to bear such a blow.

The morning after my arrival I woke early, it wasn't yet six. Matteo and Sofia's house, where I was staying, was silent even though I was sure I wasn't the only one awake. I wasn't feeling good, I had a bellyache. When I got to the bathroom I cursed menstruation.

No baby for Marco and me. It was certainly a punishment for all those times I had breathed a sigh of relief when I saw the red blood in my panties. I was a failed mother, bereft of a child I never conceived, and widow of its father.

I went back to New York, uncoupled. I discovered I didn't have a home anymore. Our wonderful apartment was still there, but it was no longer my refuge, my nest, the place where I could let myself go, safe in the arms of my love. With Marco I had always been free to be myself, without raising barriers, putting on a front or being defensive. Now all this was finished. Over and done with.

I made an inventory of everything that had belonged to him, with no witness. I laid his suits on the bed, his shirts, jeans and T-shirts, shoes and many other things. I selected what I would keep forever and gave the rest away. I took possession of his collection of sunglasses and spent a day trying them on in front of the mirror, crying and laughing depending on the memories that washed over me in waves.

Marco had seen to everything: the bank and insurance papers were in perfect order, all in my name; I had no hitch, no problem. There was also the famous list of passwords I hadn't wanted to know about; I turned on his computer and found the e-mails he had exchanged with my mother. So many!

Marco told her that it would have been difficult for me, but I would have managed because I was smart and tough. I was Anna of steel, even though I didn't know it. He had written, 'Anna is most beautiful thing in my life and I'd like her to be mine always, but she must be free to start over, to move on even without me.'

And then I found myself holding the receipt for his frozen sperm. Yet again, he had made the idea return to mind. A child for Marco and me was a concrete possibility. We had discussed this many times recently and our positions were reversed. Now I was the one who wanted what I had rejected before. He, instead, had told me he didn't want it, yet... In the end, he left his sperm.

# 32
## MY LAST YEAR IN NEW YORK

*New York, May 29, 2016*

I fight, I cling to the torpor of sleep that is unraveling into a drowse. I barely move in the gray eddy on the brink of awakening. I hang on to the side of dreams; I don't want to leave this place.

Yet there is something, an energy pushing against me that decides the matter: the room resounds with a flat thump. I stretch on the couch and feel for the box of tissues. Now it's on the floor together with the book. *The House of the Spirits* is lying open, upside down, on the wooden floor.

A cramp wrings my calf, I massage it, my body curled up and stiff, and to take my mind off this I review the collection of picture frames arranged in a row on the occasional table: images of happy moments with Marco. In two photos he is with his nephews Mattia and Michele, the sons of Matteo and Sofia. They have the same smile, the same shape eyes, and even their mouths are similar; all the generations of the Falcionis look alike, as if made from the same mold. I smile at Marco, worn down by numbness. What is my life now? Sometimes I feel I don't count, I merely fill a space. I taste the wine left in the glass—it's like slop—then I pick up the box of tissues and throw it far away.

I am ashamed that I'm still at this point: anger, rancor. Yet I have even moved houses to feel safe from memories; they follow me with no malice and console me when they come like fuzzy recollections, but if I relive my days with Marco, the most beautiful moments, I break once more. Even places and objects, certain songs or an old movie and even the shows we liked to watch on television have a special significance for me. Thousands of things or situations trigger nostalgia that often reopens the wound just when I feel I'm on the mend.

Time passes, but it doesn't increase the distance between Marco and me.

Then there is the matter of the baby. That baby I still want, maybe. Marco no longer. I still have time to decide; he won't object now.

"It's not a good thing to have a child without a father. I don't want my child to grow up without me. Don't do it, Anna." How many times had I heard that in the last year? I had felt powerless, exhausted, even old. Then he had left me and it's already been three years since we two...

Anyway, now I can decide without letting myself be conditioned by anyone.

It's not true.

Marco still talks to me. He follows me and guides me in important decisions.

It's the middle of the night—I might as well sleep on it. On the bed, instead of Marco, the iPad is waiting for me. I always read the latest news from Italy before I sleep.

"You know, Marco, I'm going to think about it a bit longer," I speak to him, as I often do. "This doesn't mean I'm going to do what you want. I might even make your child." I smile as I undress. "He would be beautiful, you know. He would look like you."

Or maybe this child will remain an unfulfilled desire. A dream of my widowhood.

Widowhood—what a horrible word. A woman without her man, lost forever. I still can't describe my solitude, probably because, without Marco, for a long time I have been nothing.

Sleeping is still a problem, maybe it always will be. Sometimes I am granted a mercy and I sink into the arms of Morpheus for a few hours, only to wake up terrified and stunned by the idea that he has abandoned me. But I've stopped thinking that without Marco I would cease to exist. Immediately after his death, in the evenings I would slip between the sheets in the company of solitude and desperation, but now my only companions were nostalgia and regret.

But I am here, I am alive. I could still change my whole life, play a new hand. I keep our checks for a million dollars; I might cash them one day. After all, life is in my debt and I will not content myself with a consolation prize. I am a New Yorker and I expect the best. Marco would say that my best is yet to come, that I must have faith in change and be at peace with that part of my life I lived with him. My beautiful past.

I could go somewhere else, to start over. I see once more the blonde woman and her son who a few hours ago were admiring the perfect sunset offered by Manhattan.

Dazed by tiredness I take the path of sleep and, with a vague thought in my head, I slip into a dream. It's a perfect day and I'm strolling along 42nd Street: the sky is blue and orange, the air still yet clean, there are no cars, only people and lots of children. Everyone is smiling. My head is light; I feel that life is no longer a prison made of memories. I am wearing a serpent's skin and I am in Bryant Park. Nonchalant, I move among the people, passing from one group to another, chatting. The skin begins to flake off, it falls apart and then turns to dust, but I don't notice.

Marco is sitting on our bench. At a certain point he greets me with a wave, smiles and leaves me alone.

Right there.

*Marco with his friends in Fano (2006).*
*On the left, Marco on dad's truck (1983) and Anna poses for a "Tut-tiFrutti" advertisement (1984).*

*Marco and Anna for the first time in Camponogara (2007).*

*The ecstasy of Anna at the Grand Canyon (2009).*
*Photo by Tommaso Zauli.*

*At the altar (2010).*
*Photo on the right by Marian Vanzetto.*

*Raise your hands: the wedding (2010).*
*Photo by Amaneraphoto.*

*The last day of the honey-moon in Viareggio (2010). Photo by Marian Vanzetto.*

*The last wish, the night before Marco's passing (2013).*
*On the left, the first anniversary in Bryant Park (2011). Photo by*
*Aida Krgin.*

*Anna in Central Park (2017).*
*Photo by Margherita Mirabella.*

*Anna by the subway on Central Park West (2017).*
*Photo by Margherita Mirabella.*

*Anna in Bushwick (2017).*
*Photo by Margherita Mirabella.*

*Anna in her New York City: should I stay or should I go?*
*Photo by Margherita Mirabella.*

309

# ACKNOWLEDGEMENTS

Thank you, Mom and Dad, for going along with my wishes and allowing me to travel and discover the world since I was small.

Thanks CP – Carmine Pappagallo – for giving me a chance and changing my life.

Thanks Ilaria, for all the hours you devoted to me on Skype and for always having the right words, at the right time.

Thanks Virginia, for coming into my life like a hurricane and for literally saving me from myself.

Thanks Susanna, for having told this story with great refinement.

Thanks Marco! Without you I would never have become the woman I am today.

Annalisa M.


A special thank you to my editor, Nicoletta Molinari, first and foremost an infinitely patient friend.

Susanna D.C.

# THE AUTHORS

Annalisa Menin, narrator and blogger, lives and works in New York. Born in Dolo, near Venice, globetrotting traveler curious about life, in 2006 at just over twenty she arrived in the Big Apple and, a new migrant 2.0, she began working for Valentino, the renowned Italian fashion house. There she met Marco, the man she was to marry and to whom she has dedicated this book. New York became their city. In 2013 her husband died at only thirty-three. In his memory today Annalisa runs the initiative Remembering Marco, which finances study grants for deserving students at the Università Politecnica delle Marche, who are offered internships with Valentino USA. A part of the income from sales of this book will go to supporting this project.

Blog: www.ilmioultimoannoanewyork.com
Site: www.annalisamenin.com
Contact: ilmioultimoannoanewyork@gmail.com

Susanna De Ciechi, author and ghost writer, lives and works between Milan and Valle d'Intelvi, north of Como. As a ghost writer she has produced novels, autobiographies and memoires. Apart from *My Last Year in New York*, she has published *La bambina con il fucile* (@uxiliaBooks, 2016), based on a true story, and *Il Paese dei tarocchi,* a collective novel written with the Gli Spiumati group. In 2015 she published *La regola dell'eccesso* and *Tessa e basta* and before that she contributed to some short story anthologies, *Metropolis,* (various authors) and *Quello che sapevamo di Eliana,* (various authors).

Site and blog: www.iltuoghostwriter.it
Contact: susanna.deciechi@gmail.com

# Notes

[1] Voghera is the birthplace of designer Valentino Garavani.
[2] The reference is to Laura and George Bush, then president of the United States.
[4] *A Pocketful of Miracles*, 1961, directed by Frank Capra.